OUTSMART
YOUR EXAMS

31 Test-Taking Strategies
For Top Grades

William Wadsworth

ISBN: 9781983119699

Cover design by: Rebecca Pitt

CONTENTS

INTRODUCTION

You've got exams coming up.

Weeks, months, maybe even years of work...

... and it all comes down to this.

It's exam time.

Will it be your time to shine, to show 'em what you're really capable of?

For many students, the answer, sadly, is no.

And it breaks my heart to see, because no matter how much they pore over their books, they don't know how to deliver the goods when it counts most. For them, it doesn't seem fair that so much studying – dozens, hundreds, even thousands of hours of work – comes down to how you perform in just a handful of hours.

A few short hours in the exam hall, in which they all-too-often find themselves faltering, failing and winding up frustrated and under-fulfilled after all that feverish effort.

I don't want that to be your story.

And it doesn't have to be.

Because for a few smart students, the exam represents the time they enjoy a secret advantage, a time when they turn every single element of the exam-taking experience in their favour.

When you master these techniques, exams become the time when you performed at the very top of your game.

When you mastered your mindset.

Developed relentless energy and focus.

Made Every. Single. Second. Count.

When you maximised your memory recall and found a way through solving tricky problems.

When no matter what the examiner threw at you, you were ready with the right strategy to figure out a solution.

And at the end of it all, with your results in your hand, you are able to look back on those few short hours in the exam hall with a glow in your heart and a smile on your face.

Because you *nailed it.*

You rose to the challenge, did yourself justice, and delivered a result you can be proud of – today, tomorrow, and in some small way, for the rest of your life.

Ready to find out how?

My promise to you: a higher exam score

There is a myriad of ways an exam can go wrong.

This book will help you sidestep many of the most common pitfalls, and score higher as a result.

But more than that: we'll be putting every single aspect of taking an exam under the microscope, discovering how the right approach in all of these areas can really help you to hoover up swathes of extra marks on the big day.

This book teaches a universal set of techniques that you can make use of, no matter what kind of exam you're taking.

And no matter what state your preparations are in, I can help you raise your game:

- If you've studied well and prepared thoroughly for your exams, you'll learn how to maximise your chance of securing every single mark you deserve through good exam-week discipline and canny exam-hall tactics. From my experience, I expect many readers will be able to add enough extra points to lift themselves over a grade boundary, turning a good result to a truly great one.

- If you're feeling under-prepared for upcoming exams, on the other hand, this book can still help you. You'll learn how to be greedy for marks, optimising how you invest time and energy through exam week and in the exam hall to make sure you scrape together as many marks as you possibly can. Executed well, these techniques could help you pull a "pass" out of the bag. Just make sure you make a commitment to yourself that you'll start work earlier next time!

I'm a psychologist by training (Cambridge University). In researching this book, I distilled decades of scientific research on how memory works, and years of extensive studies on how high-performers of all kinds – from athletes to musicians – learn to cope with adversity and thrive in stressful situations.

I've spent thousands of hours talking to teachers, professors and high-achieving students as part of my work as an exam success coach – so trust me when I say I've seen it all before, and have learned the steps that *actually work* when it comes to scoring big on exam day.

And my own exam track record wasn't bad either. I graduated with a First-Class degree from university, following a full-house of ten A-star grades at GCSE, aged 15, and six A-grades at A-level, aged 17. (That put me in the top 0.01% of UK students.)

In this book, I'll share the secrets of success that I've been teaching my coaching clients for years: for the first time, making the full set of strategies accessible to anyone.

With *Outsmart Your Exams*, you'll learn how to:

- Crush exam-week nerves with the ultimate "winner's mindset"

- Develop the ultimate exam-week master schedule to make sure you do the perfect preparation routine, every day

- Eliminate uncertainty with a bespoke gameplan for every paper

- Keep mind and body match-fit and primed to perform

- Maximise your mark by reading, choosing and decoding questions skilfully

- Wow the examiner by writing answers that exude "top student" status

- Deploy smart tactics to win as many marks off the examiner as possible when the going gets tough

- Take your memory recall to new levels with a procedure for digging hard-to-remember facts out of your memory

For the most part, this book does not focus on the process of learning and studying, with the exception of one last review the day or two before the exam. So if you've still got time to get some serious studying done, check out the Exam Study Expert blog[1] or podcast[2] to make sure you're using truly effective,

---

[1] Start with examstudyexpert.com/memorisation-techniques-for-exams
[2] Available on Apple Podcasts, Spotify, or most other places good podcasts are found (search for the "Exam Study Expert" podcast). Try starting with Episode 3.

science-backed learning techniques, and getting maximum results for the study time you invest.

Outsmart Your Exams is organised into 31 Steps, each packed with the advice you need to handle a specific moment in exam week:

- Steps 1-10 deal with preparation for the exam, how to manage your time and energy through exam week, and the art of developing a killer gameplan for each paper.

- Steps 11-16 cover the period from the night before the exam through to the moment you open your paper in the exam hall. This includes getting a great night's sleep, your exam-day morning routine, and approaches for staying calm and positive before the exam begins.

- Finally, Steps 17-31 break down the core principles of great exam technique: reading, choosing and decoding questions; making your exam paper shine in the examiner's eyes; memory tricks to boost your recall; and surviving and thriving in difficult circumstances.

You're just 31 steps from the results of your dreams – are you with me?

Then turn the page, and let's *do* this!

Oh, and... I'm a Brit, and so I sometimes talk about "revising" for exams. You might say "reviewing". I also say "maths", with an "s". Let's stay friends and not worry about it too much 😊

THE FOUR FOUNDATIONAL PRINCIPLES FOR OUTSMARTING YOUR EXAMS

As I was putting this book together, I found myself coming back to four interrelated themes time and time again, whatever stage of the exam-taking process I was writing about. It's useful to take a moment to make these four principles explicit, and explain why I place so much importance on each of them, and why you should too.

You'll spot one or more of these themes running through most of the 31 specific steps that follow.

Principle One: The Aggregation of Marginal Gains

Let me take you back to 1996.

You might not even have been born then; I was six. Like the majority of the Olympic efforts of my home country, Great Britain, our national track cycling team was an embarrassment, not picking up a single medal in the 1996 Athens Olympics.

But fast forward twelve years, and the team had been transformed into a seemingly unstoppable global force. In the three Olympic Games that followed – Beijing 2008, London 2012 and Rio 2016 – the team won a total of 32 track cycling medals, of which 20 were gold.

A truly remarkable turnaround.

The team has been widely reported in press interviews over the years as attributing this astonishing success to a principle they call the "Aggregation of Marginal Gains". Simply put, that means they didn't only focus on the big, obvious advantages – like selecting the tallest, strongest riders, or making them train hard – but also on all the little advantages they could find in every last aspect of what goes into making a medal-winning performance.

This apparently includes such crazy details as:

- Discouraging riders from so much as walking to the shops and back in between training sessions, so as to rest their legs and help them recover.

- Reducing the chance of catching bugs by having surgeons train them to wash their hands to operating-theatre standard.

- Having riders bring their own pillow and coffee machine from home to the hotel they stayed in during competitions, so they could be guaranteed a great night's sleep, and would be able to start the day feeling great, with a cup of coffee just how they like it.

Previously, these issues were usually seen as too small, too insignificant to worry about.

So, they were ignored.

But add up dozens, even hundreds, of these gains, and together, they meant an emphatic winning margin on race day.

There are plenty of lessons to take from this as students preparing for exams. Some of the suggestions in the following pages may strike you as insignificant – marginal – but together, they add up to a very significant overall advantage. For instance, you'll learn:

- Techniques for saving time in the exam, for example by going easy on the fizzy drinks and coffees before the exam and avoiding a bathroom break, or by signalling to the invigilator that you need more paper ahead of the moment you actually run out;

- Techniques for maximising your writing stamina in the exam, for example, through considering your choice of pen, and even how you hold it, and;

- Techniques for reducing the risk of being derailed by something big, like being late to the exam, by planning a reliable timekeeping "safety net" and allowing plenty of time for your journey to the exam.

Add up these modest advantages and the dozens more like them, and you're able to give yourself a pretty significant performance boost in the exam.

Principle Two: The Elimination of Surprise

Surprise is the enemy of success: forewarned, you can be forearmed.

A number of the suggestions that follow are about eliminating as much uncertainty as possible through good exam-week discipline.

Because these problems seem so unlikely to occur, many students won't bother to do anything about them. As a consequence, many fall foul of easily-avoidable errors every single year.

A powerful way to eliminate (or nearly eliminate) the chance of overlooking something important is by using a checklist. The simple checklist may sound like a rather basic tool, but it's a tool used to great effect by people in a whole range of high-pressure situations, where the cost of a mistake can be substantial.

Hospitals that use checklists have lower infection rates because they make far fewer mistakes in treatment.

Pilots that use checklists fly safer planes because they are far less likely to make errors that can compromise safety.

And the Japanese trains or New York subway cars that are operated using checklists run with fewer delays.

You'll find a number of checklists through this book: checklists to help you turn up in the right exam with the right kit, checklists for making sure your exam gets underway smoothly without hiccups, even checklists for checking your paper for errors when you're done. Using these lists will simultaneously improve your performance, and also increase your confidence that everything is OK, thereby decreasing your anxiety.

The "Elimination of Surprise" is about more than just checklists, though: it's an overarching philosophy for reducing uncertainty in all aspects of exam week. For example:

- How much time will you allocate to final preparations for different subjects?

- In which order will you tackle the questions in the exam itself?

- How much time do you allocate to different sections?

Different techniques here can lead to very different outcomes, and you need to know ahead of time which will be most advantageous to you, so you're not taken by surprise on the day.

Principle Three: Going the Extra Mile

Others can be good, you'll be better.

I don't want you to jump to the conclusion that going the extra mile is about burning the midnight oil through exam week; this isn't about working all hours and turning up exhausted, with bags under your eyes for each paper. As per the principle of the Aggregation of Marginal Gains, exam week should feature plenty of sleep and an early stopping time each night, so you are as fresh as you can be for each paper.

But there *are* plenty of places you can look for a rarely-walked extra mile, that won't cause you to deplete your energy reserves too much.

In the run-up to each exam, it's about preparing diligently, working "smart", not hard, in your final preparations for each paper to make your course content as fresh and accessible as possible on the big day.

In the exam itself, it's about being greedier, thirstier, hungrier than most others, and pushing yourself (and your brain) in ways that most[3] don't bother to do.

- Many lose focus and all but stop working in the last fifteen minutes of an exam: you'll keep going, and earning marks right to the end.

- Many see questions that look hard and give up on them too soon: you'll learn strategies in this book for wrestling with tough questions, and wringing as many marks out of them as you can.

- Many settle for "good enough": you'll keep checking and double-checking your work for as long as there's time on the clock.

- And many will start to relax towards the end of exam week: you'll maintain drive and discipline right to the final paper.

No matter whether you're aiming to scrape a "C" or soar through with an "A double star", keep striving, and don't settle

---

[3] Or at least, most average students... if you're in a more competitive class, particularly at university level, you may have a rather different experience and find that "pushing yourself" is the norm!

for any less than the absolute maximum number of marks you can achieve.

Principle Four: Look for Unfair Advantages

If you do what everyone else does, you'll get what everyone else gets.

Find unfair advantages, and exploit them.

The three principles we've covered so far – the Aggregation of Marginal Gains, the Elimination of Surprise, Going The Extra Mile – are all unfair advantages, in their way.

But there's more: be receptive to new ways of doing things, new ways of thinking, and you can give yourself an edge in some surprising ways.

Outsmart Your Exams will show you techniques for using the materials provided to you in the exam – rough paper, the exam script itself, even the contents of your stationery case – to give yourself such powerful advantages they can almost feel like cheating, even though they are (and always will be) perfectly within the letter and spirit of the rules of the exam hall.

And you'll learn what goes on in your brain when you try and recall a piece of information, and how you can "hack" that process to remember facts, figures and formulas you might otherwise have forgotten. Not a substitute for studying properly for the exam, but a useful supporting technique to help get everything possible out of your memory and onto your answer paper.

It's Time To Claim Your Bonuses

This book represents one half of a complete system designed to maximise your mark on exam day.

The other half is the *Outsmart Your Exams Companion Pack*, which contains key templates, exercises and cheat sheets referred to throughout this book.

Using both the book and the *Companion Pack* together will give you the best possible shot at success, while saving you valuable time through ready-to-print / ready-to-fill-in-digitally templates to make preparing for exam success ultra-quick.

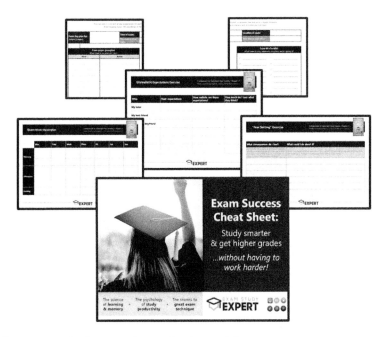

See examstudyexpert.com/outsmart-bonuses

It's packed with all the goodies you need to get the most out of this book, including:

- An **Exam Day Gameplan template** (ready to print or fill in digitally) – the plan you need to make sure every moment in the exam counts.

- The **On-The-Day Checklist template** – eliminate unnecessary stress from exam day by being extra-sure nothing gets forgotten.

- Your **Exam Week Masterplan template** – don't get caught out, map out how you'll spend and conserve both time and energy right the way through exam week if you're facing multiple exams.

- My **"Unrealistic Expectations"** and **"Fear Setting"** exercise outlines to help you conquer your demons, overcome nerves and master your exam-day mindset.

As well as my **signature Exam Success Cheat Sheet** – all you need to know about studying for your exams the *smart* way, so you can learn faster, remember more, and get your prep work done in less time than ever before.

And the best news is the *Outsmart Your Exams Companion Pack* is completely free to you, as a reader of this book!

[FREE] To download your copy of the *Outsmart Your Exams Companion Pack*, head right on over to:

examstudyexpert.com/outsmart-bonuses

Why not head right to the link above to grab it now, before you forget?

And when you're ready, I'll see you right back here.

It's time for Step 1.

1. SHIFT INTO EXAM-TAKING GEAR

"If you don't do your revision properly, you know what'll happen? YOU SHALL NOT PASS!"

– Sir Ian McKellen, channelling Gandalf from Tolkien's Lord of the Rings when speaking to students at a high school in Somerset, England

Hopefully you *have* done your revision properly – this book isn't intended to be a "Get Marks Quick" shortcut to good grades without doing any work. (Though as I said in the introduction, if you're feeling under-prepared, hang in there – I may yet be able to help you claw over a grade boundary or two on the day with a bit of good strategy).

As you get within a couple of days of your first paper, you'll need to shift out of "revision gear" and into "exam-taking gear". As you navigate the gear-shift, take stock of how your revision has gone.

Are you feeling on top of each subject?

It's a rare student who would categorically answer "yes" across every paper. There's always that topic you find tough, that subject you're worried about, or perhaps you're simply feeling a little anxious across the board.

Start to make peace with these worries. You don't have to aim for perfection in the exams, just do the best you can. You can still get a great grade (even a top grade) without scoring full marks on the paper. I'm not saying give up if there's still time to put things right, but if you're about to hit exam week, it may be time to start letting go, and move your gaze from individual topics to the bigger picture.

Address any bad habits you slipped into in revision season. It's never a good idea to trade a good night's sleep and good health in exchange for extra hours at your desk through the night. This is especially true when you've got exams to sit: you'll need to conserve your energy so you're fresh, alert and creative for each paper. Your priority in exam week is to be well-rested and alert for the exams themselves (see Step 5 "Looking after number one", for more on taking care of yourself).

Athletes often "taper" before a race or competition: that means gradually stepping down the intensity of their training in the run-up to the big day, to make sure they are as fit and fresh as possible for the race. Too much last-minute training, and they'll be exhausted and unable to perform at their best.

This is the time to ease off the pressure, save your energy for the exams themselves, and focus on consolidating what you know. Reviewing material throughout exam week is an important discipline, but you've got to be strategic in how you invest your precious time at this stage. Planning is key: the next Step will show you how.

2. YOUR EXAM WEEK MASTERPLAN

"Failing to prepare is preparing to fail."

– Benjamin Franklin, scientist, author and Founding Father of the United States

No student should enter exam week without a well-made exam schedule by their side. It's not only about making sure you're cool, calm and at the right exam hall at the right time, it's also about building in the perfect amount of final prep time for each exam. Doing that well needs a bit of careful thought.

Exam week overview

Nothing can unravel your hard work faster than turning up late or in the wrong place to an exam.

Get a copy of your exam timetable as early as possible, and find an hour at some point to develop an exam week masterplan from it. A good time for this exercise is when you've done about as much studying as you can take for the day.

The first step is to create a more visual overview of exam week: something that allows you to see at a glance how your exams are spaced, and where the gaps are between the exams. See the example below, with the exam papers, times and locations marked up for a student taking exams in Maths, Chemistry, Physics, French and Music[4]:

	Mon 23rd	Tues 24th	Weds 25th	Thurs 26th	Fri 27th	Sat 28th	Sun 29th
Morning					9–10.30 FRENCH Writing Sports Hall		
Afternoon		2–5 MATHS 1 Sports Hall	2–5 FRENCH Reading + Listening Sports Hall	2–3 MUSIC performance Music Room	2–4 CHEM. PRACTICAL Chemistry Lab 3		
Evening							

	Mon 30th	Tues 31st	Weds 1st	Thurs 2nd	Fri 3rd
Morning	9–12 PHYSICS 1 Sports Hall	9–12 MATHS 2 Sports Hall	11am FRENCH Speaking MFL3		
Afternoon		2–5 MUSIC Sports Hall			2–5 PHYSICS 2 Sports Hall
Evening					

To save you some time, I've made a printable template for this that you can download directly at examstudyexpert.com/outsmart-bonuses.

But template or no template, double- and triple-check you've got everything right on your timetable: right paper, right date, right time, right place.

---

[4] This probably won't look quite like your exam timetable – different students around the world will have different numbers of papers for different subjects. You might have done your practical exams (e.g. French Speaking or Music Performance) long before your main "exam week". Your afternoon exams might start at 1pm not 2pm. No need to write in – the principles this example illustrates will still apply 😊

Building your safety net

Once you've got this far, make a couple of copies of your timetable to use as your exam "fail-safe system". Everyone benefits from a safety net, to as-good-as-eliminate your chances of being late for the exam or missing it altogether.

If you live with your family – and consider them trustworthy! – hand a copy of this timetable over, and ask them to check you're running on time for each exam. If you live alone, perhaps you could pre-set all your exam alarms on your phone, or arrange to have a close relative or (reliable) friend phone you to check in before each exam, to make certain you're up in time.

You know yourself best: the more often you miss appointments, run late for trains or forget things, the more important it is for you to have a robust safety net in place.

Planning your final preparations

Many students get this far then stop. But I'm a huge fan of going further and planning how to spend time *outside* exams through exam week. A well-formulated "masterplan" for these final preparations can make your exam week, just as a bad plan, or the absence of one, can cost you.

Your time in exam week will be severely limited: you shouldn't be compromising on time for sleeping or eating, and you'll need at least a little time to pause for breath after each paper. Deduct the hours you'll be spending travelling to and from the exams, not to mention taking them, and you won't be left with many hours to complete your final round of study for each paper.

Your time is not only limited, it's also valuable: a final review of the right material the day before an exam could make all the difference to making something you need to know stick in your short-term memory, or not[5].

So how you invest those precious hours in exam week really matters.

Timetabling your final preparations in advance means you don't need to burden your brain with extra decisions during

---

[5] Again, this is not an excuse to avoid studying properly: this strategy is best used to complement a good programme of study in the weeks leading up to the exam. Feverish cramming the day before is always best avoided. If you need convincing, here are 3 reasons:

- Cramming won't always work: even if it has worked for you in the past, as your course materials get ever harder and more complex as the years go by, your luck will eventually run out and you'll find yourself unable to cover the material you need in the time you've left yourself. By the time you've realised, it will be too late!
- Cramming doesn't set you up for long-term academic success: increasingly, you'll find your courses and classes need to draw on what you learned in previous years. Crammed knowledge is temporary: quickly gained, quickly lost. Knowledge built up through spaced learning over several weeks or months is far more durable (see examstudyexpert.com/ebbinghaus-forgetting-curve/ for an explanation of what spaced learning is and how to do it effectively).
- Cramming is risky: if you're ill or something unexpected happens the day before, when you're supposed to be doing all that cramming, you're in trouble – there's no margin of safety.

Of course, if it's too late this year, then do what you can for now, and do your best – but make a commitment to yourself that you'll be better next time!

exam week: you know what you need to do and when, you just need to execute your plan. Advance planning also lets you look ahead to pre-empt "crunches": it's not always the best idea to prepare only for tomorrow's exams, and if you have a busy and complicated schedule, it might not always be obvious how to prioritise your time.

So, take your exam week schedule, and using a different coloured ink to the colour you used for exams themselves, mark up exactly what subjects you want to do final prep for, and when.

Here's what a well-thought-out plan might look like, to illustrate some of the factors you'll need to consider and the choices you might need to make. This one is for an imaginary final-year high school student sitting exams in French, Maths, Music, Chemistry and Physics:

	Mon 23rd	Tues 24th	Weds 25th	Thurs 26th	Fri 27th	Sat 28th	Sun 29th
Morning	Maths 1	Maths 1	French Reading + Listening	9-10.30 Chem Practical / 10.30-11 Music Warm-Up	9-10.30 FRENCH Writing Sports Hall / 11-12 Chem Practical	French Speaking / Physics 1	Physics 1
Afternoon	French Reading + Listening	2-5 MATHS 1 Sports Hall	2-5 FRENCH Reading + Listening Sports Hall	2-3 MUSIC performance Music Room / French Writing	2-4 CHEM. PRACTICAL Chemistry Lab 3	Maths	Maths / Music
Evening	Music Practice	Music Practice	Music Practice	French Writing	Night off!	Music	Physics 1

	Mon 30th	Tues 31st	Weds 1st	Thurs 2nd	Fri 3rd
Morning	9-12 PHYSICS 1 Sports Hall	9-12 MATHS 2 Sports Hall	French Speaking / 11am FRENCH Speaking MFL3	Physics 2	Physics 2
Afternoon	2.30-4 Maths 2 / 4.30-6 Music	2-5 MUSIC Sports Hall	Physics 2	Physics 2	2-5 PHYSICS 2 Sports Hall
Evening	7-8 Maths 2	French Speaking	Night off!	Physics 2	☺

This student clearly runs a tight ship, and is an example to us all. Let's walk through each day, and unpack what she's planning to do and why:

- **Monday 23rd:** with Maths 1 the next afternoon, it would be easy to get drawn into the trap of spending a full day-and-a-half preparing for Maths, but looking further ahead, there's French and Music, both with only half a day's prep time. So, she's spending the morning on Maths, the afternoon on French, and taking an hour in the evening to do some practice for the Music performance, which she finds a relatively low-stress way to end the day.

- **Tuesday 24th:** the morning of an afternoon exam is usually best spent getting ready for that exam, so it's a final look over Maths in the morning. Some more Music in the evening after the Maths exam.

- **Wednesday 25th:** final French prep before her paper that afternoon, and a final evening practising for Music.

- **Thursday 26th:** she's using the morning to get ahead on Chemistry Practical prep for Friday afternoon, as otherwise there will barely be any time for Chemistry once her Friday morning French paper is done. A last warm-up before her Music recital, and that evening, final French Writing prep for her exam the next morning.

- **Friday 27th:** the week closes out with the first "double day", but she takes it all in her stride, knocking out French Writing in the morning, and taking a final look through the Chemistry Practical materials straight afterwards. A double day can use up quite a lot of energy, and with a couple of days before the next paper, a well-earned break is in order tonight to recharge.

- **Saturday 28th – Sunday 29th:** an ill-prepared student could fall into the trap of looking ahead to only the next exam, and spending the weekend on Physics. But that would create a pretty sticky Monday afternoon, trying to work up Maths 2, Music and French Speaking all at once. So our student does the sensible thing, and spends the weekend balancing her final prep for Physics on Monday with getting ahead on prep for Tuesday's Maths and Music, and Wednesday's French.

- **Monday 30th:** after the morning Physics exam, she's free to divide the afternoon between Maths and Music for Tuesday. Having spent a good amount of time over the weekend on both of these subjects, Monday afternoon is a relatively low-stress affair.

- **Tuesday 31st:** a long but hopefully satisfying day in the exam room, with an hour in the evening for a final reminder of materials for French Speaking.

- **Wednesday 1st – Friday 3rd:** Once this last French paper is out of the way, Physics 2 is the only paper that remains. She's got the luxury of time, and makes the smart move of capitalising on that time rather than wasting it. A break is definitely in order on Wednesday night following a couple of tough days, but otherwise, she stays focused on the prize.

It can be hard to keep going right to the end, especially if other students have already finished exams, but go the extra mile at times like this, and you will be rewarded.

There is some flexibility in this plan, but not a tonne. If you decide to change things too much today, you might create bigger problems for yourself tomorrow. So, if you find you're not getting through your final prep for one subject fast enough, modulate your work pace accordingly, and try to fit the work into the time you've got available.

That may mean you don't have time to do everything you wanted for each subject: prioritise spending time on topics that come up a lot, rather than more peripheral ones.

Your exam week masterplan will be a great foundation for success if you execute it well, making the relevant course material as fresh as possible in your mind for each exam, and helping you stay calm and in control throughout exam week.

3. A GAMEPLAN FOR EACH EXAM

"The secret of success is to do the common things uncommonly well."

– John D. Rockefeller, widely considered the richest man in modern history

You've got your masterplan for exam week: you're in control of the big picture. Now you need to focus in on the details, and develop a gameplan for each exam.

Top tennis players think about the specific tactics and strategies they want to use against each opponent: that's their gameplan. You too should you have a set of gameplans for your exams, so you know exactly what you're doing in each exam.

You've got a strictly limited time in the exam to show the examiner what you're capable of, and you'll be nervous, so you need to think carefully in advance about how you want to divide up the time – don't trust yourself to get it right by winging it on the day. Make that critical time-allocation and work-order decision in advance, and test your approach through mock papers, so you know the plan works, and that you can rely on it.

Initial scouting

First, you'll need to know the exam format:

- What sections are there?

- How many marks is each section worth?

- What topic(s) does each section cover? (if applicable)

- What style are the questions – e.g. an essay / short answer questions / multiple choice?

- Do you get a choice of questions?

Use this information to map out the structure of each paper you're taking – let's say this is your upcoming Pogonology[6] Paper:

	What	Marks
Section A	Short answer questions on all topics – no choice	40
Section B	Choice of 3 essays on Topics P, Q, R	30
Section C	Choice of 3 essays on Topic X, Y, Z	30

---

[6] The study of beards, if you were wondering (bet you were). Anyone know any pogonologists? Tweet me @ExamStudyExpert, it would make my day…

What to include in your game-plan

Once you know *what* you need to do, figure out *how* you'll do it.

A good rule-of-thumb is to allocate time allowed for each section in proportion to the marks awarded per section: many students know this, but most won't go any further in their preparations. You can go the extra mile. Consider:

A. How much time you'll need to check the format and rubric
The "rubric" is the instructions on the front of the paper that tell you what sections you need to answer, and whether you have a choice of questions. You should read the rubric on the front when you enter the exam hall, but by that stage it should be a case of simply confirming the structure is exactly as you expect it – there shouldn't be any surprises here to you.

B. How long you need to choose and plan essay questions
If you've got complex essay questions to answer, don't skimp on planning.

Examiners are looking for well-structured answers that deliver logical and coherent arguments, and launching into an essay without a plan makes this very difficult to deliver. Without a plan, you run the risk of writing a "stream of consciousness" style answer, which may cost you marks for writing style. Alternatively, you may try to carry the structure of your essay in your head as you go, but that blocks up vital mental capacity, and means you risk remembering less about the topic.

Time invested planning is time very well spent: for in-depth essays at university level, for example, I'd suggest allowing at least 25% of the total time allotted to the essay for your plan. So, for a one-hour essay, give your plan a full fifteen minutes.

C.   Whether you need a plan at all

You might not need a plan if you're a strong student facing a more "predictable" essay-based exam, by which I mean, one where the questions tend to be quite similar to ones you've tackled before. You might find this earlier in your academic career, for example, in middle school or in GCSEs (UK exams taken age 16). If you're already very comfortable with what you need to say, perhaps your time is best served by diving straight in, particularly if you have a considerable amount to write under substantial time pressure.

But treat a decision *not* to plan your essays with caution: it can carry more risk. In particular, be absolutely sure you've understood the question you are answering in the exam, and are engaging with it fully (see Step 20).

So, to plan or not to plan? The only way to know for sure is to try it both ways under timed conditions, and discuss the pros and cons of both approaches with your teacher or tutor.

D.   What order to work in

How would you tackle that Pogonology paper?

You need to do some short answer questions (Section A) and two essays (Section B and C). Some students would simply work through the paper in order – an approach I call the "first things first" approach:

The "first things first" approach:

Many students will make a slight improvement on the "first things first" approach by looking ahead at their essay questions before they tackle the short answer questions – if only because they're anxious to check that there is an essay they feel comfortable tackling:

The "look ahead" approach:

Finally, the student that is really on top of his or her game would adopt the best approach of all:

The "outsmart" approach:

So why do I recommend the "outsmart" approach? Three reasons:

1. The start of the exam is when you are at your most fresh, with adrenaline pumping and your mind rattling with ideas. Take advantage of that, and get your essays planned out while productivity and creativity are at their highest. You will be feeling tired later on in the exam

(particularly if it's a 3-hour monster) and will be glad of having already done most of the hard work.

2. A set of essay plans to carry you through the paper is an invaluable safety net in case things go wrong. If you are running short of time, getting stressed, getting tired, it all doesn't matter quite so much if you have a decent essay plan in front of you to work from. All you need to do is write up the plan.

3. Most cunningly, by getting your mental juices flowing on the details of the essay topics right at the start of the exam, you'll find that – somewhere deep in the back of your mind – your brain will spend the intervening time turning the topic over, rooting around for extra facts, clarifying structure, and even coming up with useful ways of phrasing things. In other words, while you're working on your short answer questions (as in the pogonology exam), you will be subconsciously preparing for the essays to come, making them that much easier to write up when the time comes.

When I sat final exams at Cambridge, I had three papers, each of them three-hour, three-essay papers. That meant one hour per essay: of which 15 minutes was planning, 45 minutes was for writing up in neat. I'd start each paper by writing all three plans, so 45 minutes into an exam, I'd have three plans written, but not a word of an essay. The person next to me might have nearly finished their first essay.

That's a terrifying place to be if you're not used to it: but have faith in the gameplan you decided on and the rationale for it, and stick to your guns.

No essays to plan? Fine – but is there a notoriously tricky last question or two on the paper? Could you take a read of that before you go back to the start and begin working through the paper in order? That way you get to take advantage of the third benefit mentioned above: that of allowing your brain to subconsciously chew over the problem, and start coming up with some solutions while you're working on the front half of the paper.

E. An alternative approach for the more nervous student

The approach of starting, in effect, with the tougher parts of the exam might not be right for you in all circumstances. If you're a naturally nervous candidate, or it's a paper you're particularly worried about, there could be something to be said for an alternative philosophy which prioritises putting you at your ease: perhaps flicking through a few pages of the paper to find a nice "friendly" question to make sure you get off on the right foot.

Getting an early win under your belt could be just the thing to help you relax and find your groove in the exam hall.

F. How long to leave at the end for checking your work

The final element to consider is how long you want to spend reviewing and checking what you've written.

For me, this depended on the paper – if it's a problem-based paper where a silly mistake early in a calculation might derail a whole question, it's a wise investment of time to double-check your workings. For essay-based papers, I usually found limited value in checking back over my essays – I'd got the info down as intended, I often couldn't improve the mark much with a check-through, and the time was best spent thinking of and writing down more relevant points.

A definite exception would be essay papers where the accuracy and quality of your language itself carries a lot of marks, such as in an English Language paper, especially if you are prone to spelling / grammar mistakes. Same would go for foreign language papers and translation exercises.

See Step 30 for more on checking techniques.

Putting it all together

Who knew there could be such depth to the simple question of what order to do your exam in, and how long to spend on each section?

Let's apply all of that to our Pogonology Paper and see what we might come up with:

	What	Marks
Section A	Short answer questions on all topics – no choice	40
Section B	Choice of 3 essays on Topics P, Q, R	30
Section C	Choice of 3 essays on Topic X, Y, Z	30

Time	What
0900-0902	Check structure and format is as expected
0903-0905	Choose essay questions for Sections B and C
0905-0920	Write plan for Section B
0920-0935	Write plan for Section C
0935-1020	Section A
1020-1105	Write Section B essay
1105-1150	Write Section C essay
1150-1200	Time to check work / cushion time if behind on essays

Phew – a lot to remember, never mind the contents of the topic. The trick is to practise with it before the day – put yourself through a number of timed papers using this format to help it become second nature.

Make checking over your gameplan part of your final preparation for each paper, and if it's complicated like this one, consider writing down your plan when you get into the exam hall to help you stick to it. You don't want to have "trying to remember gameplan" as an extra mental burden during your paper – write it down, and free up mental capacity.

As a minimum, try to commit a couple of key times from your gameplan to memory. From the example above, these might include "0935", the time you should start Section A, having chosen and planned essays for Section B and Section C, as well as "1020", the time you should move on from Section A and start your two essays.

It's worth pointing out that you don't need to do B and C in order, you might like to start with the one you think you'll pick up marks on most easily, to make sure you do yourself justice.

Having a plan like this means you're not leaving anything to chance on the day – no surprises. You know how long you've got for each element, and you know those timings work because you've tested them. You're allocating your time in the most efficient way possible, giving yourself the best possible chance of picking up all the marks you deserve in each section, and reducing the risk of running behind.

All that said, while I believe it's vital to have thought out and tested your gameplan in advance, that doesn't mean there isn't space for a little wiggle-room – there's always a few minutes leeway either way.

And of course, your good judgement on the day may deem it necessary to deviate more drastically from the established gameplan timings. More on this in Step 16: The Starting Gun and Step 24: The Clock.

4. How to Cheat (Legally!)

"Power's not given to you. You have to take it."

– Beyoncé, 100 million record selling artist

Alongside planning timings in your gameplan, it may also be helpful to think ahead to the resources you'll have access to in the exam, and how you want to use them: whether you're bringing in notes you've prepared in advance, making your own cheat-sheet in the exam itself, or using materials that the examiner provides to you.

"Bring your own" notes

It's rare these days, but sometimes you're allowed to take notes into the exam. Make the most of it, by writing these as early as you can in your preparation process, and using them while you work through practice papers. Every student can take the notes in, but the smart students looking to go the extra mile will ensure the quality of their notes is second to none.

Continually refine your notes to ensure they are as useful as they can be, in line with your changing understanding about how to nail that subject. If space is at a premium (e.g. you're only allowed one A4 sheet), don't waste a drop – commit easy-to-remember facts to memory so that they don't need to take up valuable real-estate on your page of notes.

"Legal" cheating: unofficial cheat-sheets

Even if you can't take notes into your exam, you may find it helpful to write out a "cheat-sheet" of key information when the exam starts, which you can refer back to for the rest of the paper.

- For some A-level Maths papers, for example, I practised writing out all the key formulas for that exam on a single piece of paper. Took me about four minutes.

- In a Physics exam, this might mean scribbling out a skeleton electromagnetic spectrum, and a few tables with the basic circuit laws in.

- For Language papers, this might mean making a note of tenses, when they're used and how they're formed.

- For Music, it might be key signatures or a keyboard to work out intervals.

With your cheat-sheet to hand, you'll be much more relaxed for the rest of the paper – you'll already have some of the facts you will need at your fingertips, relieving some anxiety, and freeing your brain from having to recall information, allowing more capacity for problem-solving.

Besides, it's sometimes much easier to remember this kind of information as an inter-related chart or table: sets of Maths formulas that go together, or tables of grammar. Recalling just one piece of information from the table is tricky, and you'll be more prone to making an error. But writing out the full table can sometimes virtually guarantee you've remembered it all accurately.

Think once, write it down, and get it right for the rest of the paper.

The key to making this work is to practise in advance, and get used to doing it quickly – if scribbling out your cheat-sheet takes you longer than five minutes, it may be too detailed.

Always lay out the cheat-sheet in the same way, to help trigger your memory of what goes where.

And to avoid any risk that you might look to be breaking exam rules, be sure not to start writing your cheat-sheet out until after the invigilator invites you to start the paper.

Be clever in using the resources in the exam hall

Most students who use cheat-sheets write them on blank paper: that's absolutely fine, and works great for lots of people.

But if you're struggling to commit the cheat-sheet to memory, I've known some students go a step further and learn to write it on something you have access to when you're revising, and that the examiner freely gives you on exam day: the front cover of the exam paper itself.

The cover is almost always the same, with text laid out in the same place on the page, and generally, the same language used for the rubric. You could learn to use this as a source of unfair advantage, using the exam cover to cue your memory of the components of your cheat-sheet:

- Learn to put each section of your cheat-sheet in a different white space on the front of the exam.

- Look for clues or memory cues in the text of the rubric itself: for example, a set of three words in the rubric that start with the same letters as the symbols of a formula you need to remember.

Thinking further still outside the box, I've even known students use the contents of their stationery case as memory cues.

I'm not talking about taking in notes of any kind: that *is* cheating, and not allowed.

But you can take as many pens and pencils of different colours as you like into the exam: a set of these could help you remember something you need to know. How about a set of 7 coloured pens to symbolise the 7 major parts of the electromagnetic spectrum, for example: each colour of pen representing one part of the spectrum. Practise putting the pens in colour order, and training your memory to associate each colour with all of the relevant knowledge of the properties of that part of the spectrum.

Formula booklets and other reference materials

Finally, don't neglect the help that the examiner wants to give you.

Many exams will provide you with some form of reference materials. Formula booklets are common for many exams in Maths and Sciences, particularly at higher levels, while some language papers will provide a copy of the relevant book, play or other literature that is being examined.

You may decide the formula booklet has everything in it that you need, or you may decide you need to learn a little more, and develop your own cheat-sheet to top it up.

Perhaps you could train yourself to write the "top up" notes on the formula booklet itself (if you're allowed to write on it), next to the formulas from the same theme.

Ensure you are familiar with the reference materials before you get into the exam – know exactly what you can expect to find in them, and learn to navigate your way round them so you don't waste time in the exam.

5. LOOK AFTER NUMBER ONE

"If you think taking care of yourself is selfish, change your mind."

– Ann Richards, former Governor of Texas

After all that effort planning your exam week strategy, it would be a shame if you weren't on top form when the time comes. The next couple of steps will help make sure you're in the best physical, mental and emotional shape to shine on the big day.

Healthy body, healthy mind

You'll be demanding a lot of your mind and body in exam week, so make sure you're putting the right fuel in the tank.

- **Eat well.** This isn't a nutrition book, so I'll keep it simple. A very rough starter guide is to make your plate half vegetables, preferably a couple of different types (spinach, broccoli, carrots, peas, kale, cauliflower, green beans etc.); one quarter carbs (rice, pasta, potatoes etc.); one quarter protein (fish, meat, eggs, soy etc.). Don't take on too much processed food or too many ready-meals if you can avoid it.

- **Stay hydrated.** This means with water: real water, on its own, not combined with other things (so no, tea and coffee don't count!). Keep a bottle of water on you, and get in the habit of sipping regularly. You can tell if you're properly hydrated when you're producing pale straw-coloured urine every few hours. If you need to go frequently and it's colourless, drink a little more slowly. If it's dark yellow, drink more[7].

- **Watch the sugar.** You find sugar in all sorts of treats (chocolate, biscuits, cakes, sweets) and drinks (fizzy colas, lemonade etc.). A bit of a treat in exam time is OK, but too much will play havoc with your blood sugar and energy levels, so go easy.

- **Caffeinate with care.** Like too much sugar, too much caffeine can cause your energy levels to swing about. Worse, the adrenaline rush you will get from exam-day nerves can be compounded by caffeine, making you feel jittery and anxious. If you don't rely on tea or coffee to get you through the day, you might want to cut it out completely for exam week. If you're one of those people that simply can't face life without the black stuff, keep it in your routine, but enjoy in moderation, and not too late in the day (see Step 12 for more on the effects of caffeine on sleep).

- **Avoid supplements.** There are a whole range of brain-boosters on the market – pills to give you better memory, pills to make you more alert, pills to make you write faster, pills to factorise quadratic equations for you[8]. I'd advise against these: your brain is a delicate beast, and foreign chemicals could easily have unwanted, poorly understood

---

[7] Yep, I'm talking about wee. Oh, come on – no sniggering at the back!
[8] OK, I might have made that last one up...

side effects. So at best, you could be wasting your money; at worst, there's a real chance you'll be impairing your abilities in the exam.

Finally, for those of you of legal drinking age in your country, I'd suggest keeping a clear head by cutting out alcohol for exam week.

Keep yourself off the sick-bed

Remember the British cycling team and the Aggregation of Marginal Gains? The steps taken to keep riders healthy are quite extraordinary: cleaners wipe down door-handles in hotel rooms and lifts when the team is away at competitions; riders follow a highly specialised nutrition programme; and they bring their own pillows – and sometimes even their own beds – to make sure they sleep well.

It's all about maintaining a healthy, race-fit body, giving them the best possible shot at glory.

You might also want to consider taking steps to avoid illness and injury:

- Consider dropping out of contact or high-risk sports (like skiing, rugby or American football) for exam week, to reduce your risk of broken bones.

- If it's winter, go slowly on the ice – don't rush anywhere.

- Wash your hands thoroughly in warm soapy water after using the bathroom and before eating.

- Get a good night's sleep every night (see Step 12).

If you do get ill or injured, don't panic. If you're well enough to work, it's likely that your preparation and the adrenaline of the exam will carry you through.

In borderline cases where you can drag yourself to the exam room but your performance is substantially affected, you may be able to apply for an extra mark allowance to compensate – see Step 29, and discuss the problem with your school or college exams officer.

And if you really can't sit the exam, there are always options, from re-entering the exam in a later cohort, to being awarded a grade or degree based on your record of good coursework and classwork[9].

Focus on the prize

Try to keep the rest of your life ticking over with minimal attention, so you're free to focus on preparing for, taking, and recovering from exams.

If you have a part-time job, can you take holiday for exam week, to leave you free to focus on your studies? If taking a break from work is going to be financially difficult for you, do you have any relatives who would be prepared to support your academic

---

[9] Another reason to study steadily through the year, rather than leaving it all to a last-minute cram!

ambitions, and who could help you with expenses for a week or two[10]?

During an intense exam week, you won't have much time to socialise. Try and find a way to dial back social and family commitments without alienating people – don't preach to your friends about how they should be working, just get on and do your thing, and make your excuses cheerfully and without a fuss.

Ignore anyone who gives you a hard time for being a swot: those close to you should be understanding if you can't be your usual sociable self for a spell.

There's an old metaphor of crabs in a bucket, trying to escape: if the crabs were to help each other up, letting one another stand on their shoulders, at least some of them could escape. But the crabs at the bottom keep pulling the climbers down: if the bottom-crabs can't escape, they're not prepared to let the climbers out either. So all the crabs stay in the bucket.

People who don't think they can succeed (or often, who can't be bothered to put in the effort), will sometimes try to block their friends from succeeding too: "if I can't pull myself out of the bucket, I'm certainly not going to let you climb out either."

If you're surrounded by people who keep pulling you back down into the bucket, you need to find a way to cut them loose.

_____

[10] I know that's not going to be possible for everyone.

Find people who will help you climb out of the bucket, if you can, but at the very least don't let yourself be held back.

Finally (as far as you can!) try to avoid major life changes around exam time. I know you can't always control what life throws your way, but if you are facing major events like moving to a new house or starting / ending a relationship, and have an option to delay for a couple of weeks until after exams, take it.

6. KEEP YOUR COOL

"Everything will be okay in the end. If it's not okay, it's not the end."

– John Lennon, lead singer and songwriter for The Beatles

Exams can be stressful times.

Our brains evolved to respond to dangers in the environment – like a threatening sabre-toothed cat – by making us breathe faster and our heart pound, priming us to either run away or to fight. To our prehistoric brains, an upcoming test or exam looks just like a "danger", and the body responds in the only way it knows how: your heart rate goes up, and your palms sweat.

That's anxiety.

It can be a real barrier to success in exams: but the good news is, there are some simple strategies you can use to get your "caveman" mind to relax.

A. Flip the narrative

Most of us assume that any physical sensations of being nervous – like sweating, or a racing heart – come as a result of the emotional feeling of nerves. Actually, science shows us that the chain of causality is the other way round: the physical reaction (the sweating or the racing heart) comes first, the brain adds the emotional interpretation (nervousness) second.

But here's the thing: the things your body does when it's nervous are very similar to the physical sensations of being excited. So use that to your advantage, and flip the narrative.

Train yourself to re-interpret that pounding heart as a sign that you're not anxious, but excited: not worried, but instead, primed and ready to perform at your best.

B. *Walk and smile*

You can take this idea further, and force your body to create physical signals that the brain has little choice but to interpret positively. Walking and smiling are two great examples. If you're walking gently, physical threat must be a long way away: your brain interprets a steady stroll as a sign that all is well.

Chewing gum works in a similar way: you wouldn't be eating at a time when you're facing danger, reasons your brain, so everything must be OK.

You could even try smiling more and seeing if you feel happier: crack a grin, and even if you weren't feeling much like grinning at first, you might find yourself feeling a touch more cheerful afterwards.

C. *And, breathe...*

Breathing deeply and gently from your belly is a great way to find calm: a few slow breaths like this as you open your test paper will do wonders to steady your nerves. And if anxiety is getting to you on your way to the test, do some slow breathing while trying a grounding exercise: engage with one sound, one sight and one smell in your surroundings as you breathe slowly.

Mindfulness meditation takes this principle further, and is a fantastic practice not only for bringing anxiety under control, but also for developing deeper focus[11].

D.   Work it out

Exercise can be a great way to relieve pent-up tension. Try and get some most days when you're revising for exams.

If you're not a natural athlete and struggle with the idea of sport and exercise in general, perhaps you could go for a brisk walk?

E.   It's OK to be nervous

Finally, don't be too hard on yourself: it's perfectly normal to be nervous for a big test or exam. Don't expect to eliminate anxiety altogether: the trick is in how you cope with those nerves. Follow these five strategies, and you should be well on your way to finding a calmer frame of mind.

* * *

Remember, this does not constitute medical advice. If you find you're having serious problems with anxiety, see your school counsellor or your doctor.

---

[11] Read more about the benefits of meditation on my blog at examstudyexpert.com/benefits-of-meditation-for-students/.

7. CRUSH YOUR DEMONS

"Whether you think you can or whether you think you can't, you're right."

– Henry Ford, founder of the Ford Motor Company and sixth richest man in modern history

In my experience, the tension people feel about exams can often be explained by a mismatch between the expectations you (or others) are putting on you, and what you think you'll be able to achieve.

To address this, you've got two choices: a) being better-prepared or b) lowering those expectations.

You might already be working as hard as is sensible, in which case, you're going to be as well-prepared as you can be.

That only leaves (b) as the sensible solution. Consider investing some time to examine the weight of expectation on you. High expectations are all very well if they are spurring you on to your best work, but if they are getting in the way of a healthy relationship with your studies, it may be time to address those expectations, and tone them down to something more appropriate.

Identifying unrealistic expectations

Try this exercise: grab a piece of paper, and fill in a table something like this:

Who?	What grades do they expect me to get in the exams?	How likely am I to get those grades?	If I'm honest, how important is their opinion to me?
My tutor			
My best friend			
Girlfriend / boyfriend			
Mum			
Dad			
Me			(Very important, surely?!)

Alternatively, to save you a few moments, you can head to examstudyexpert.com/outsmart-bonuses to download a printable template copy of this table as part of your free companion pack that accompanies this book.

Once you've got your table, start to assess the implications. You can dismiss unrealistic expectations quite easily if they come from someone whose opinion you don't care about too much.

So, who's left? Whose unrealistic expectations are giving you the most problems?

Parents are a common culprit – they may be fiercely proud of you, and want the best for you. Communication is the key: ask them for a chat, and explain how you're feeling. "Mum, I'm getting quite worried about the exams – and I'm getting so anxious sometimes that I feel I'm losing focus. I think a big reason I'm getting so anxious is because I want to make you happy – can we talk about it?"

"Fear-setting" for students

But the biggest critic of ourselves is often... ourselves! The expectations you place on yourself are often the hardest to deal with.

Roman philosopher Seneca the Younger taught that confronting fear head-on can be a good way to tame it.

Are you getting stressed over crazy-ambitious targets? Write down what your targets are, even if you haven't admitted them properly to yourself before now. Then ask yourself, how bad will it be if I *don't* hit these targets? What's the worst that can happen?

Try this exercise, inspired by Seneca. Take a sheet of paper, and divide it into two columns:

- Label your first column "what consequences do I fear?" and write down all of your fears about the consequences of not hitting your exam goals.
- Label your second column "what could I do about it?" and here, think through what you'd actually do if that scenario came to pass.

Here's an example to show you the sort of thing I mean:

What consequences do I fear?	What could I do about it?
	• I could always retake the exams • If I take a year out to retake the exams, I'll have time to travel Africa like I'd always wanted
• I won't get to the college / career I want	• I could go to my second-choice college, which may be better suited to me anyway -- so I'll be happier when I'm there • Switch tack and be an entrepreneur and be even wealthier / more fulfilled than if I'd taken a conventional career
• Less self-esteem / respect from parents / others	• I could find new sources of self esteem or respect: in sport, music, business, fitness...
• Feel like effort has been wasted	• Know that I've learned new things • Know that I've developed new skills (writing / speaking / analysis / resilience / problem-solving...) • Know that I've made lasting friendships

Whatever disasters you're envisaging, once you start thinking them through carefully, they'll start to not look so bad after all. Maybe you'll miss out on your first-choice university. So what? You'll still get to go to a great university, work with some great tutors, have a brilliant time and leave with some strong job prospects.

Whatever happens, the world isn't going to end.

Exams are not the only route to success.

And if your worries are still getting to you, make sure you find someone you can talk to about it: your college nurse, a counsellor, your doctor. Some 18% of people will suffer from some kind of anxiety-related disorder every year, so help is available if you need it.

Things are going to be OK in the end.

8. PLAY BY THE RULES

"N.B. – Do not on any account attempt to write on both sides of the paper at once."

— *W.C. Sellar, "1066 and All That: A Memorable History of England"*

One source of anxiety in the exam itself is being unclear on the rules. The good news is that this is very easy to solve, through a little prior thought and preparation.

Having confidence that you're doing things right is much better than looking over your shoulder in doubt the whole time, worrying whether you're about to get your knuckles rapped by an irate invigilator.

Rules are in place to level the playing field, making sure everyone takes the exam under the same circumstances, and giving everyone the same shot at success.

Some common rules

I don't know your rules, but here are a few common things to consider:

- What are you supposed to wear?

- What kind of writing implement do you need? Some multiple-choice papers demand black biro, or pencil.

- Are you allowed to drink water? (I hope so!)

- Are you allowed to bring discreet snacks? If so, what? Most exam halls would say "no": even if it was allowed, I never did.

- How far in advance are you supposed to arrive? Doors might open fifteen minutes before the start time: arrive after this time and it might feel like you were late, even if, technically, you weren't.

- Are you allowed a calculator? If so, what kind?

- Do you need to leave rough paper behind at the end of the exam? Don't fold or crumple any materials in the exam, so it's clear nothing has been taken out of your pocket.

You certainly won't be allowed phones, smartwatches or any other electronic devices beyond a simple watch or approved calculator. It's the big one – get caught with a phone in the exam, even if it's off, and you'll face steep penalties.

Check what your exam rules are, and if anything is unclear, speak to your teacher or tutor before exam day.

Play fair

We discussed "legal" ways to cheat back in Step 4. That was all a bit of fun: seriously, please don't *actually* cheat.

You know what cheating is: it's accessing information during the exam other than from the neurons in your head. I don't care how ingenious or foolproof your system is, it's simply not worth being caught.

The consequences can be severe – worst case, you could be thrown out of not just your current paper, but of all your other subjects too. That leaves you without the set of qualifications you were working towards, jeopardising your academic and professional future.

But perhaps most importantly of all, it's not ethical: I'd hope my readers are the sort of people who would aspire to leave the world a better place than they found it, in some small way, and one of the best steps to take towards that is by conducting yourself with integrity and honour.

9. TOOLS OF TITANS

"A woodsman was once asked, 'What would you do if you had just five minutes to chop down a tree?' He answered, 'I would spend the first two and a half minutes sharpening my axe."

– Anonymous woodsman, popularly attributed to Abraham Lincoln

Even if the list only has "pens and water" on it, it's still worth taking a moment to ensure you've got everything you need to see you through exam week to avoid last-minute stress. Have you got *enough* pens? Do you know where your water bottle is?

Stock check

Cut yourself a little time a few days before your exams start in order to assemble your exam kit, and to make sure you've got the stocks you need to see you through. This might include:

- Two different alarm clocks to wake you up on the morning of your exams – tested and reliable.

- The necessary stationery for all exams you will be sitting – pens, pencils, rulers, and so on. A decent rubber is often handy to correct mistakes if you might have graphs or diagrams to draw.

- Something to carry your stationery in, which is within regulations – that often means a clear / transparent case.

- A watch to tell the time in the exam, just in case you are far from the official exam clock, or if, like me, you find it much easier to make sense of passing time from an analogue watch face (clocks in large exam halls are often digital).

- An approved style of calculator (if you need one), with memory wiped before each exam.

- Spares for anything essential – spare pens, spare pencils, spare calculator batteries.

- A bottle of water to take into the exam.

Your water will be nicer if you've kept it in a cool spot (i.e. the fridge) beforehand rather than leaving it out in the sun all morning[12].

Identify what you've got and what's missing, and make yourself a shopping list.

Kit checklist

I'd suggest making a physical checklist for each of your exams. That way, you can physically tick off everything in the morning as you leave the house, eliminating the chance you miss something. It's the Principle of the Elimination of Surprise in action again.

---

[12] Hey, there aren't many other luxuries you can give yourself in an exam, but a sip of chilled water is one of them...

Among the printable exam prep resources[13], I've got a template sheet for each paper you sit, which combines your exam gameplan with a kit checklist on a single page, so you can see at a glance everything you need to remember for and about this exam. If you've got lots of different requirements for the different papers – a calculator for one, a set square for another, your paintbrushes for a third – you can adapt the checklist for each paper accordingly.

Include on your checklist everything you need to make the journey to the exam (travel cards, money), and anything you might need when you arrive (some exams need an ID card).

If all this sounds overly fussy, remember, it's all about finding marginal gains in minimising the risk of things going wrong (like not having a calculator).

If you've got a busy study schedule, incorporate this kind of admin work into your routine as breaks from work, or as activities for the evening when you've done enough work for the day. You could use an extended break from work to make your exam checklists, and if you've got anything missing, make "go shopping" into a separate break.

_____

[13] Download from examstudyexpert.com/outsmart-bonuses

Make life easier for yourself

As well as giving some thought to what you'll physically need for the exam, think about other aspects of exam week that might be made that bit easier with a little forethought.

If you take care of feeding yourself, then stock up on supplies. Get a grocery shop done, and stock the freezer with a few pre-prepared meals.

Get your room / house looking clean and tidy, so you don't have to do much housework for a week or two.

Catch up on laundry so you've got enough exam clothes to see you through. Consider buying an extra pack of socks or another shirt or two if you have to, if that will enable you to get through exam week without wasting time at the laundry room.

10. MAKE THOSE FINAL STUDY HOURS COUNT

"You can waste your lives drawing lines. Or you can live your life crossing them."

– Shonda Rhimes, showrunner of Grey's Anatomy, Scandal, How To Get Away With Murder

You've got your plans figured out, you're taking good care of yourself, you've got your exam kit figured out.

It's time to hit exam week itself.

Are you ready?

Final preparations

You've already drawn up your masterplan for what subjects you're doing, and when (Step 2): but what should you actually be doing when you sit down for your final work on each subject?

You may only have a couple of hours for your final preparations on a subject before the exam on it: what is the highest-impact way to spend that time? Unless you've got a long gap (several days) between papers, you won't have time for any more "revision work", that means you generally won't be spending time:

- Learning new things

- Making new revision materials

- Practising full papers

Instead, you'll want to:

- Go broad: review all the material for a paper or subject, rather than getting drawn too deep into one topic. Nothing wrong with dedicating half an hour to polishing a high-mark topic you are shaky on, but don't spend all afternoon on it.

- Revisit: reuse revision materials you've already made, this isn't the time to make fresh ones, save for some simple scribbling out of what you can remember about a topic from memory.

- Preserve your energy: a packed schedule of exams will demand a lot of focus and concentration. Don't exhaust yourself so much in your final preparations that you deplete your energy for the exams themselves.

Recall-based papers

For papers that rely on remembering information, the best thing to do the day before an exam is to test yourself on your revision notes or flashcards.

The best way to get information to stick *in* your memory and to make sure you can easily recall it in the exam is to practise pulling the information *out* of memory[14].

_____

[14] This is the principle of retrieval practice, and if you only know one thing about study / revision technique, it's this. For more on my No. 1 favourite

Be strict with yourself: try and remember the date, formula, translation or whatever first, and look at the answer second (no peeking!).

If you're trying to remember complex information – a list of three or more items, a diagram, or a formula with more than a few terms – you must write it down. There's a limit to how many different bits of information you can actively hold in your mind simultaneously – it's like having too many programs or browser windows open on a slow laptop, making it crash.

You need to free up capacity in your brain to remember more of the list / formula etc. – that means writing down what you've remembered so far. And as a bonus, you'll develop visual / muscle memory more easily: your hand will start to remember how a formula goes, your eye will start to remember what a diagram looks like.

Keep a separate sheet of paper to hand to make a note of anything you find hard to remember, and practise recalling these facts from memory until they stick. You could sneak a final look at this sheet before you leave the house for the exam.

You might not have time (or energy!) to test yourself on everything on the course, in which case, you'll have to prioritise. You could adopt a hybrid approach, splitting your time between "going broad" by skimming through your notes on all topics,

---

revision technique, check out examstudyexpert.com/memorisation-techniques-for-exams/

and "going deep" by testing yourself on a few high-priority topics.

Skill-based papers

Some subjects like English or Maths are skill-based, so as well as re-studying any facts you need (quotes, formulas, etc.), your final preparations should include some "warming up" for the question style in the exam.

Unless you've plenty of time between exams, you might want to avoid doing full papers under timed conditions, to avoid burning yourself out.

Find a less demanding way to warm up for the paper, and to get your thinking back into the right patterns.

If a full paper is too much, just do a few select questions.

If writing full essay answers is too much, just plan the structure and points you want to make in detail, and perhaps draft the first few paragraphs, and your conclusion.

Either way, don't choose the ridiculously challenging questions – you want to warm yourself up, not freak yourself out.

11. The Night Before

"Of course, it is very important to be sober when you take an exam. Many worthwhile careers in the street-cleansing, fruit-picking and subway-guitar-playing industries have been founded on a lack of understanding of this simple fact."

— *Terry Pratchett, "Moving Pictures"*

We're getting down to the sharp end: it's the night before the exam.

Clock off in good time

I'd suggest wrapping up your final preparations at least an hour and a half before you want to go to bed, so you've got plenty of time for a relaxing wind-down routine.

A couple of times, I made the mistake of working right up to bedtime for a paper I was nervous about, and slept terribly each time. Much better to sacrifice an extra hour or two's work (it's hard to see it making that much of a difference at that stage anyway) and make sure you are well-rested and fresh for the exam.

Hopefully not many of you will contemplate burning the midnight oil before an exam. I once knew a guy who was 30 minutes late to an exam itself because he was trying to squeeze in some last-minute revision.

This is crazy.

I've yet to be convinced of a case where the benefits of a few hours of extra low-quality, foggy late-night work outweigh the disadvantages of going into an exam with brain fuzz because you didn't get any sleep[15].

No matter how under-prepared you feel, the way to maximise your marks is by having your wits about you in the exam, following a decent sleep, rather than by trying to get extra cramming in.

Check...

Before you start to wind down, check the details for your exam tomorrow. Get your clothes and all your exam kit ready (see Step 9). Double-check where you're supposed to be, and at what time, and check travel arrangements, are as you expect them to be.

Sort out your morning wake-up call: remind yourself what time you need to be up to avoid rushing in the morning, and set your alarm. If you're using a smartphone as an alarm, make sure it's charging and on airplane mode (you don't want to be disturbed in the night).

If you live with reliable friends or family who would be happy to act as your alarm "backstop", agree the time at which they'll

---

[15] Want to debate it? Tweet me @ExamStudyExpert.

come and extract you from bed if you accidentally sleep past the alarm.

... and chill

Then it's time to chill out. Close your books and put them away, to signal to your brain that work time is over, and it can start to power down for the evening. Move to a physically different space, if you can.

I'd suggest allowing at least an hour between stopping working and going to bed. Two hours might be better.

Spend this time doing things that will soothe your mind, not agitate it. This might include:

- Reading a book: either fiction, or a non-fiction topic that's unrelated to the subject of your exams.

- Having a warm bath: the drop in body temperature after a bath may help you feel sleepy, and can help you to slow down and relax before bed.

- Gentle yoga or meditation.

- Taking a light walk outside to watch the evening sun.

- Watching a little TV if you want – though try and choose relaxing programmes you can easily call a halt to, rather than addictive box-sets that will get your heart racing and will have you tempted to binge for longer than you'd intended. I used to queue up a good nature documentary for exam week.

A restful wind-down routine is an important first step for a great night's sleep: read on for some more tips to help you get the rest you need in exam week.

12. SLEEP SCIENCE

"I love to sleep. I'd sleep all day if I could."

— *Miley Cyrus*

Your wind-down routine is a great start: here are the other practical tips you should know for sleeping well in exam week (and indeed, throughout the rest of your life!).

These are summarised from "sleep scientist" Matthew Walkden's excellent book "Why We Sleep". Check out the Bibliography for details of this book, and all the other books and scholarly articles that have informed Outsmart Your Exams.

1) **Have a regular sleep schedule:** aim for more sleep than you think you need (especially in exam time), around eight hours for most students. Wake up and go to sleep at the same time each day. Many people are used to setting an alarm to wake up in the morning: you may also benefit from an alarm that signals when bedtime is approaching, to make sure you're in bed on time.

2) **Exercise is good, but not too late in the day**: try to take your exercise earlier in the day, and avoid it two to three hours before bedtime.

3) **Caffeine is best avoided in the afternoon / evening:** it's not just in tea and coffee, you'll also find it in colas and even chocolate. The caffeine from a morning

cappuccino should largely be gone by the end of the day, but a cup of coffee after lunch is likely to leave caffeine in your system until bedtime. That makes it harder for you to fall asleep, and even when you do, the quality of that sleep will be impaired.

4) **Don't nap after 3pm:** fine before then if you need to.

5) **Keep your bedroom dark and cool:** if your bedroom isn't reasonably dark already, try putting up new curtains that don't let so much light in. Or just wear an eye mask. Keep the temperature on the cool side, if you can. If noise is disturbing you, experiment with earplugs: I preferred wax ones that cover the ear hole rather than the foam barrel ones which are inserted into the ear.

6) **Get some sun:** sunlight has a powerful regulating effect on your internal body clock. Try and aim for at least half an hour in natural sunlight each day.

7) **Go gadget-free:** just as sun during the day is helpful, you may also have heard that "blue light" emitted by smartphones, laptop screens and other devices can be very unhelpful at night. Best to avoid screens completely an hour or so before bed, but if you have to look at them, use "Night Shift" mode on your phone, or install an app to manage this for you (e.g. "Twilight" on Android phones).

8) **Don't lie wide awake in bed for too long:** if you're consistently having trouble sleeping, or you're starting to feel anxious in bed, the advice from the scientists is

to get up. Do something restful until you feel sleepy, so you don't come to associate "being in bed" with "being awake".

These tips should all help you to be well-rested and exam-fit throughout exam season. But if you're still having sleep problems – or have a bad night before a paper you're particularly anxious about – don't despair. You're probably getting more rest than you realise, and adrenaline and your preparations should be able to carry you through the paper the next day.

As with my suggestions on exam nerves / anxiety, remember this does not constitute medical advice. If in doubt about your sleep habits, consult your doctor.

13. EXAM DAY DAWNS

"There are no limits!"

– The quote on the back of the flapjacks in our college canteen. My friends and I adopted it as something of an exam-term battle cry.

Well, good morning!

Your nerves may be jangling softly, but you're in control – you've done your prep, you've got this.

Get up

I always liked to get the day off to a brilliant start with a really uplifting tune as a wake-up alarm on my phone. Personally, I liked a track with a very quiet start that just creeps into your dreams before building to a full-volume, rousing finale, so that I could get out of bed already feeling awesome.

Actually get up with your alarm – no snoozing for you today, it will only make you dozy, and it might mess up your plans for your morning routine and cause an unnecessary stress in your day.

If you struggle to wake up with an alarm as much as I do, put it on the other side of the room so you have to physically get out of bed to turn it off. Put dressing gown and slippers next to the alarm so you can jump straight into them and begin your day, reducing the temptation to slither back into bed.

Get ready

If you're the sort of person that loves to start the day with exercise to be at their best, then do that.

If you're not that sort of person (I wasn't, in my exam-taking days), then don't: maybe one day you might want to change that, but exam week isn't the time to start experimenting with new exercise rituals. Save it for later.

If you're facing a morning paper, allow yourself sufficient time to get ready – for me, that was 45 minutes to eat a decent breakfast, shower and dress, then another 10-20 minutes before leaving the house for a final glance over the material for that exam, so it was as fresh as possible in memory.

Give a final check as to what you're bringing with you: have you got all the right kit you need for your paper today? Use the checklist you made in Step 9.

Get there

A good rule of thumb is to aim to arrive fifteen minutes before the scheduled start of the exam, and assume the journey will take 50% longer than usual. So, if your journey usually takes an hour, allow 1.5 hours. If your exam is at 9am, you're aiming to arrive at 8.45am, so leave at 7.15am.

If the journey is unfamiliar, it may be a good idea to practise it in advance, so you don't have any surprises on the day.

You might enjoy listening to music or comedy that puts you in a good mood while you're travelling to your exam.

Get in

If you arrive in good time for your exam, as per your plan, you'll usually have a short wait outside the exam hall before you're called in.

It can get the nerves going at the best of times, so you want to avoid standing with friends who will shake your resolve by bragging about how much work they've done, or by reciting obscure facts just to show off.

Ideally, you want low-grade chit-chat about non-exam topics: if you can't find friends you trust to be good exam-waiting company, stick to your own company instead.

If you're under-confident on the basic facts for the paper, use this time to steal a quick final glance at a condensed page or two of notes – you might only need to remember those facts for ten minutes, and you can write them down as soon as the exam starts[16].

It's a good idea to use the bathroom in the half-hour leading up to an exam – get that out of the way now, so you can focus on your paper once the exam begins.

---

[16] As ever, NOT a substitute for studying diligently in the run-up to the exam: just a little top-up if there's something you're particularly shaky on.

14. Cultivate a Champion's Mindset

"Just believe in yourself. Even if you don't, pretend that you do and, at some point, you will."

– Venus Williams, the first African-American World No. 1 tennis player in the modern era

On your way to the exam, or while waiting outside, your main job is getting yourself into a positive mental state of mind.

Self image

It's natural to be a bit on edge – accept that. Adopting a strong mental self-image can help prime you to perform at your best.

If you're feeling confident about this paper, you might envisage yourself as a mighty warrior on your way into battle. Nothing on Earth is going to get in the way of you vanquishing any problem that stands in your way.

Or maybe a gentler self-image suits you better. You could be a gardener, tilling your vegetable patch, weeding out mistakes, and cultivating a paper of beautiful, blossoming answers.

Or you could be a doctor. Or maybe an athlete. Or a top scientist. Or a brilliant entrepreneur. Let your imagination run a little – but choose a self-image that carries a lot of potency for you, and is at once positive and reassuring. Bring your mind back to your self-image of choice whenever you find your resolve faltering.

The power of mindset

Mindset really does matter. In the American education system, African-American students have a history of underperforming academically when compared to the national average. Many people have tried to figure out why, and the full explanation is complex and still not fully understood.

It now seems that at least a part of the answer lies in mindset.

In an experiment, African-American students who were asked to write their ethnicity on the front of a test paper scored significantly fewer marks compared to students of other ethnicities. Yet when students were *not* asked to write their ethnicity on the paper, the performance differences vanished, and all students performed equally, regardless of their race.

Why?

It's been suggested that some African-American students don't associate traits such as being studious or academically successful with their own ethnic group. When they are reminded of these perceived "norms" by the simple act of writing their ethnicity on the exam paper, it seems they become less likely to call up their academic A-game, and as a result, don't hit their full potential.

Pretend you are a top student

So, even if you don't *feel* like a top achiever, pretend to yourself that you are, and try to act like one.

Ask yourself, "what would a top student do under these circumstances?"

Or, "how would a top student answer this question?"

With practice, you might just find yourself becoming the top student you set out to emulate.

15. What To Do Before The Exam Even Starts

"I do not try to dance better than anyone else. I only try to dance better than myself."

– Arianna Huffington, founder and editor-in-chief of The Huffington Post

The doors swing open.

Still feeling like a champion, I hope, you walk in.

The exam hall can be a pretty intimidating place. I've taken exams in cavernous halls filled with row upon row of little square desks, maybe approaching a thousand in total, each one home to a student just like you for the next few hours.

You might feel a flutter of nerves: take a couple of deep breaths from your belly, then find your seat and get settled in.

Pre-flight checks

Once you find your desk, make it your home – settle in, physically as well as mentally. That little table will be your world for the next one, two or three hours. At this point, switch into the routines of a seasoned exam-taker:

1. **Check** there is nothing on the table there shouldn't be – no used rough paper from a previous student,

and no paper which looks to have been folded or crumpled.

2. **Check** whether your chair or your desk rocks, and if it does, ask the invigilator for some folded paper to go under the leg.

3. Do a last **check** of all your pockets, hunting for any items which could get you into trouble. If you find any, ask an invigilator to put it at the back of the room for you.

4. **Put down** your water bottle on the floor, and keep it there for the duration of the exam, except when you're sipping from it. You don't want to have to hand in a soggy exam script because you knocked water all over it!

5. **Get out** all of the stationery you'll need, and take your calculator out of its case, all ready to go.

6. **Fill in** your candidate details on the front of the paper.

7. If you're wearing a watch and want to use it, **synchronise** it to the exam clock.

Check, check, check; put down, get out, fill in, synchronise: your pre-exam checklist.

Check the format

Finally, turn your attention to the paper in front of you: confirm it's the exam you're expecting to sit, and read the instructions carefully to verify that the structure and format of the exam is as you're expecting.

Every year, students just like you throw away vast numbers of marks by misreading the rubric. If you're meant to answer three essays and you do five, or one, you're really going to struggle to get more than a very mediocre mark, at best. So take your time, and double-check what you're supposed to be doing.

Take change in your stride: if the format's not what you were expecting, be prepared to adapt your gameplan accordingly. You've come so far, you're not going to let little things like that throw you off your stride.

16. START STRONG

"The time is one minute past nine. You may start."

– The voice of your invigilator

And so it begins.

The curtain rises: showtime.

You feel another little kick of adrenaline as you open the paper to reveal the questions inside.

With any luck, you'll discover questions about topics that seem familiar, and you can start to lay down what you know.

If not, you can get into scrambling mode to pick up as many marks as you can.

Exams aren't won in the first moments of an exam, but they can be lost. Don't charge in at 100 miles an hour and risk misinterpreting the rubric or choosing your questions unwisely.

Slow down, breathe, and get it right.

Remember your gameplan, and stick to it. We make poor decisions under stress and pressure, so don't let yourself "go rogue" and deviate wildly from the gameplan unless there's a good reason to. Whether you're feeling the magnitude of the occasion or you've got students scribbling furiously in your peripheral vision, don't let yourself be put off your carefully thought-out course of action[17].

Keep your head down, focus on your paper, your desk, the clock, and blank out everything else. Put the blinkers on, and keep them there for the duration of the exam, working only for yourself.

If your exam strategy involves writing up a cheat-sheet (see Step 4), now's the time to get it written up. If you're supposed to begin by reading and choosing questions, do that. Or if you've just decided to start from the front and work forward, get going with the first question.

Ease yourself into a steady, efficient, workmanship-like rhythm that will carry you through the exam. If you've prepared well, you might even start to enjoy it – there's a rarely-talked about satisfaction that comes from showing off what you know, and writing answers you feel really good about.

You've got this.

---

[17] There are a few valid reasons to deviate from your gameplan, however – see Step 24.

17. Understand The Life Of The Exam Hall

"The question isn't who is going to let me; it's who is going to stop me."

– Ayn Rand, novelist, playwright and screenwriter

Let's be honest with each other: exam halls are pretty strange places to hang out. I can think of very few environments with such an intense atmosphere as a room containing hundreds of students, writing furiously, in total silence.

Understanding the beat of the exam hall will help make alien circumstances feel more natural and comfortable to you on the day.

More paper

If all's going smoothly that day, asking for more paper should be about the most excitement you ever get in the middle of a paper. In a big hall, it can take a minute for an invigilator to get to you, so stick up your non-writing hand before you run out of paper, and keep writing while you're waiting, if you can.

Getting extra paper on time might free up no more than 60 seconds, but remember the Principle of The Aggregation of Marginal Gains? Those seconds will feel very precious when they are 10% of your remaining ten minutes, and you've still got a lot to say.

And don't let yourself be distracted by other students asking for paper, how much, and how soon. Some people have enormous exam handwriting...

Bathroom breaks

Staying well-hydrated is important, but don't chug so much water in the exam that you're running to the toilet all the time; if you can avoid a bathroom break, you'll gain a couple of extra marginal minutes to spend on your exam paper. Going easy on the fizzy drinks and coffees before the exam will help with this. If it's a long exam paper, your stamina might be pushed: your exam hall's "bathroom procedure" should have been explained to you, but if you're unsure, check with the invigilators.

Cheeky, but you could use a bathroom break tactically. If you're having a bad day in the exam, a bathroom break may be a good way to pick yourself back up, regain your composure, and walk back in ready to do what it takes to get through things.

Taking mini-breaks

You'll want to pause for breath occasionally in a paper, particularly in a long one. After a tough question, or when you reach a milestone like completing one of your essays, you might want to take half a minute to gather your thoughts.

Have a drink of water, close your eyes and take a couple of slow, thoughtful breaths.

Pause, find a moment's peace, and smile to yourself.

Then re-engage the engines, and return to your paper refreshed and ready to go again.

The invigilators are on your side

Invigilators are there for two reasons. First, to check everyone abides by the rules of the exam, creating a level playing field, and second, to help you with problems: escorting you on bathroom visits, helping you resolve distractions that are seriously putting you off (noise distractions, chilling draughts, etc.), as well as being a point of contact for flagging suspected mistakes in the paper.

The students are often not the only ones who wish they could be somewhere else other than the exam hall: the invigilators may often be wishing that too! Invigilation usually involves a long stint of doing nothing except watching you work.

I've heard of invigilators making up games to entertain themselves. A game where each time you walk the length of the exam hall, you must do it in fewer steps than you did previously. A "paper race", where points are won for being the first to deliver extra paper to students that need it. Even a form of human Pacman.

Don't let any of this distract you, but feel free to let the knowledge amuse you. It might just make the exam hall atmosphere feel a little less frightening and a little more friendly.

Be a good citizen of the exam hall

Finally, take note of good exam hall etiquette: basically, don't distract other people from their work.

Don't be that guy (or girl) everyone is glowering at in the exam hall: that means no despondent sighs, grunts of frustration, satisfied outbursts, crunchy crisps or violent leg jiggling.

Your friends will thank you later.

18. How To Avoid Choking Under Pressure

"And why do we fall Bruce? So we can learn to pick ourselves up."

– Thomas Wayne, Batman's Dad

Heck, we all fall – even Batman.

And it's that fear of falling, taken to extremes, that can cause us to clam up, freeze, go into mental spasm at the worst of moments.

For decades, under-prepared athletes have come within inches of winning a major tournament or game, only to snatch defeat from the jaws of victory, their game suddenly going to pieces under the pressure of what they are about to achieve. We now know that too much pressure can have a detrimental impact on all manner of performers, from Scandinavian skiers to Indian data-enterers.

For us students, it might be that the pressure of exam situations, rather than spurring us on to do our best, gets under our skin and causes us to panic and lose focus.

The good news is that it doesn't have to be this way: it's my job in this section to make sure that this isn't going to happen to you, with the help of two simple strategies.

Get out of your brain's way

If you followed the advice in Step 7 about crushing your demons, you'll have spent some time thinking through what "disaster" in an exam looks like – and realised it's not that scary after all. It may feel like the be-all and end-all now, but you've still got a fantastic life ahead of you no matter what the outcome of these exams, I promise.

So if you find your anxiety levels creeping up in an exam, take a moment to remember that. Count to five slowly, take a calm breath on each ("One… Two…. Three… Four… Five…"), letting go of tension, tightness and discomfort with each out-breath, and inhaling a feeling of warmth, and a smile.

After your five breaths, start changing the story your brain is telling itself.

Back in Step 6, "Keeping Your Cool", we talked about how emotions are a reaction to what the body is doing, not the other way round, i.e. your body's physical response comes first, rather than as a reaction to an emotion.

You have the power to re-interpret those physical signals from your body as a different feeling. We said the body does very similar things when it's anxious and when it's excited. So instead of defaulting to your brain's first interpretation – "my heart rate is increased and I'm sweating, so I must be panicking" – change the story to "my heart rate is increased, so I must be excited and ready for action"!

Encouraging your brain to interpret that state of heightened alertness as excitement, not anxiety, is sometimes all you need to take the reins again.

If you practise mindfulness, you'll find this sort of awareness and control of your thoughts comes even more naturally. There are some very good apps out now that will help you get started in just a few minutes a day, for free, like Calm or Headspace.

If you've prepared well for your exams, use that to rationalise with yourself. "I've been working sensibly towards these exams for weeks / months, I'm as well prepared as I could expect to be. If I'm finding this tough, lots of others will be too – I just need to do my best, find marks wherever I can, and get through it."

Inoculate yourself

What can you do to make sure all this is going to work before you get into the exam room?

The secret is to practise in stressful situations before the exam. Find ways to ramp up the stakes in artificial situations:

- If you get the opportunity to take mock exams, brilliant. If not, perhaps you could engineer one: ask someone whose opinion matters to you (like a teacher / tutor / supervisor) to set and mark a practice paper.

- Do this practice under timed conditions, ideally in a studious environment with lots of other people working silently, like a study room or library reading room.

- Replicate conditions in the exam as closely as you can: use a real exam script (as far as possible), the real formula booklet, the calculator you'll have on the day, the stationery you plan on using. Even wear similar clothes to the ones you'll be in on exam day if you can.

Part of replicating conditions as closely as possible is to "Eliminate Surprise" (remember Principle Two?) – you don't want to use your exam calculator or pen for the first time on the big day, only to find you don't know a crucial function, or the pen makes your hand hurt.

But perhaps more importantly, this is about working through your fears before the big day: the more you can get comfortable with the conditions of the exam, the easier it will be on exam day itself. If you need to ramp up the pressure further, try committing in advance to sharing your results with people whose opinions you respect.

Get used to performing when you feel the weight of expectation on you, then by the time the real exam comes round, you'll be ready to handle anything.

19. Bring Your A-Game

"Thank you, Mr. Examiner, I'm HAVING that mark!"

– Gordon Prescott, my Chemistry teacher

If you're handling the pressure of the exam, you've won half the mindset battle: the other half is developing your thirst for success. As you work through the exam paper, hunt down every last mark you possibly can within the time available.

Go the extra mile: let nothing stop you from getting the score you deserve.

It seems like strange advice to need to give, but students, particularly younger students, often stop at "good enough", rather than striving for "the absolute best I can do" in exams.

I think it comes down to confidence in large part – confidence that if you strive, you will be rewarded.

Be greedy for marks, and you'll get more of them.

Leave no stone unturned

Thirst voraciously after every possible point you can win:

- When you feel in control of a question, aim to bust out a knock-it-out-of-the-park full-mark score. Go above and beyond (as far as the available time permits) to really show the examiner what you're capable of.

- When you're not sure, scratch diligently to pick up all possible marks even if you're not going to get a full answer. There's always scope to pick up method marks, marks for the basics, even just a mark for selecting the right formula – make sure you don't leave any points on the table.

- No blanks, ever – even if you feel clueless, have a guess and write down a related phrase or two.

Going for gold

Your teachers or course leader will have dropped plenty of hints about what criteria unlock top marks – remember them, and try to use them. Here are some common ones:

- A well-structured answer

- A concise answer

- Well-explained, evidence-based logic and reasoning

- More advanced grammar / language structures (for language papers)

- Accurate use of technical terminology

- Command of dates and names

Beyond that, the right attitude for "going for gold" can depend on the subject you're being examined on.

For scientists, stick with what you know. It is a rare exam that tries to trick you, to pull the wool over your eyes, to bamboozle you or confuse you. Examiners want to see what you know, they want to give you the opportunity to demonstrate your knowledge and skill on the subject. So don't make random leaps of faith, stick with the core concepts and principles you know to be true.

For arts students, almost the opposite advice holds: be bold. This generally isn't necessary (or expected) earlier on in your academic career, but certainly, by the time you reach university / college, boldness is vital to unlocking top marks. Make sure boldness is grounded in the facts, and be sure to differentiate between what is known to be true and your own opinions. Aim to craft arguments that are different to the norm, allowing you to step away from the pack, and to show you are a cut above the rest. Back all this up with rich supporting evidence and the examiner will lap it up.

Don't slip up

The final but crucial component of your A-game should be not throwing marks away by making careless mistakes. The following tips should help you to avoid common "banana skins" that may trip you up if you're not careful:

- Always give your answer in the format the examiner requests it in.

- Make sure you give the units after scientific calculations.

- Avoid doing too many calculations in one line or skipping logical steps – at best, not clear for the examiner, at worst, you'll make mistakes (see Step 23 for more on this).

- Be sure to answer all relevant parts of each question, and answer all questions on the paper – have you checked the back page?

The more prone you are to slip-ups, the more important it is to leave plenty of time at the end of the paper to come back and check your work with fresh eyes (Step 30).

Perhaps the biggest risk of slip-ups comes from misreading the question in the first place. Read on to learn how to avoid that.

20. Ninja Question-Reading Tactics

"When the going gets tough, take it easy and slow down."

– Michael Bassey Johnson, author

Under exam pressure, it's surprisingly easy to misread questions, overlooking some crucial piece of information that holds the key to solving the problem, or even missing the point of the question entirely.

Oh, so you think you know how to read?

Sure, but over your academic career, you might read thousands of exam questions, and the chances of you misreading at least a handful of them are pretty significant.

Learning to be a master question-reader who interprets every question accurately is a "Marginal Gain" well worth having.

How you read

Have you ever wondered what happens when you read?

Your eyes aren't moving in a continuous flow, taking in each word at a time. They actually move in jumps[18], focusing every few words. Your brain fills in the words in your peripheral vision, the ones around the word you focused on, based on a

---

[18] Each jump is called a "saccade", if you're wondering.

combination of the visual shape of the word and its linguistic context (content and meaning).

The faster you read, the fewer words your eye will focus on – perhaps down to just a handful of words per paragraph when you're at full reading pace in a novel.

But because you don't focus on every single word, it's not a failsafe system.

Try reading this:

A JOURNEY OF A THOUSAND MILES
STARTS WITH A SINGLE STEP

Did you spot it?

Once you see both "As" – "a journey of a thousand miles starts with **a a** single step" – you can't believe you didn't always notice it was there! This nicely illustrates the shortcuts your brain takes when you're reading: this is exactly how you can misread or misunderstand questions.

I've had very bright students in my workshops who will miss the duplication when asked to read this aloud from the projection screen. Perhaps the slight stress of being asked to read something in front of peers impairs their performance – though you may be under a little stress in the exam too, so best to learn how to handle it, and read accurately regardless.

Be a tortoise, not a hare

The cure for this is simple: slow down, and force your eyes to process each word individually.

The most robust way to do that is to follow the sentence with your pen, highlighting key words as you go. I liked to underline key information that I would need to answer the question, and put a box round instructions about what to do.

Here's an example to illustrate what I mean:

Solar cells convert solar energy to useful electrical energy in the road sign with an efficiency of 4.0%.
The solar-cell supply used by the engineer has a total surface area of 32 cm^2.

Calculate the minimum intensity, in W m^{-2}, of the sunlight needed to provide the minimum current of 75 mA to the road sign when it has a resistance of $6.0 \, \Omega$.

[3 marks]

The "underline and box" approach will:

- Eliminate the risk that you misunderstand or misread the question.

- Improve your comprehension of the question, so you take in more of what it's asking and are more likely to understand what you need to do to answer it.

- Let key question terms pop out at you – in the example above, there are four underlined numerical terms that you'll probably need to put into an equation. The extra visual emphasis (the underlining) gives a small shortcut to the right equation by removing any mental strain in picking the key terms out of the paragraph.

- Help you refer back swiftly to the question at any point should you need to check instructions or data provided.

Don't believe me?

Researchers have demonstrated the impact of emphasising key words in a question. In an experiment, students were given a statistics question which asked "what is the probability that a chocolate picked at random is not faulty". Only 8% got it right.

The question was changed subtly, so that the word "not" was in bold typeface: and 31% got it right.

Three times as many students got the question right: that's a *massive* improvement!

So, leave nothing to chance: add your own emphasis to questions by underlining and boxing, and make sure you understand everything you need to do.

21. Choose Wisely

"Look for your choices, pick the best one, and then go with it."

– Pat Riley, three-time NBA Coach of the Year

Exams will often feature a choice of questions, sometimes towards the end of the paper, sometimes throughout.

Picking the right question to tackle is a major strategic decision to make.

What to consider when you're selecting

Question choice comes down to:

- Topics you find enjoyable or interesting vs those you don't

- Topics you know or understand vs those you don't

- Questions that look "standard" vs those that look a little more avant-garde

What you like and what you know are different things – you might have enjoyed a topic, but have few relevant facts at your fingertips to address the specific question asked, in which case you'd be better off choosing a less interesting question which you can say more about.

"Standard", familiar-looking questions can be a safe bet, but at higher levels (university) they may also be seen as lower-risk by your examiner, and can sometimes offer less potential for achieving the highest marks. Don't write off the more avant-garde options immediately – they may look harder to you, but chances are they will be looking harder to most students, and could be a route to a really good mark if you feel you have something interesting to say. Higher risk, but potentially higher gain, if you are in control of the material for that topic.

Scoring and choosing

Read through every question option, using the underlining-while-reading approach from Step 20 to make sure you have fully understood what's being asked in each.

I then rate each option using a simple scale of ticks, crosses and question marks:

- ✓✓ – dream question, yes please, let's do this

- ✓ – this looks fine

- ✓? – probably OK

- x? – not looking good, but could make something of it if I had to

- xx – definitely not

This usually makes your choice clear.

Sometimes a question will virtually leap off the page at you screaming "pick me!" – perhaps a topic you revised in particularly fine detail, happen to know quite a lot about, or just find particularly interesting. You've been handed the question of your dreams; get on with it!

Often, it will be a close call between a couple of questions. If the answer isn't worth too many marks and you're facing substantial time pressure, make a decision quickly and commit to it.

But if you're faced with a very close call and there are a lot of marks resting on the choice, it could be worth investing a little extra time in making your selection. Try spending a couple of minutes planning out each essay in skeleton form. It will usually become apparent quite quickly that you have more relevant material for one title than the other. Decide which horse you're going to back within five minutes or so, then carry on where you left off with your chosen essay title.

22. GET INSIDE THE EXAMINER'S HEAD

"Good things come to people who wait, but better things come to those who go out and get them."

– Anon.

As you're reading – and sometimes, choosing – questions, it's important to understand what the examiner wants. I now want to take you deeper into the art of reading the examiner's mind, because it's such an important part of good exam technique.

When they wrote this question, what exactly were they trying to test? What points are they likely to have down on the mark scheme?

You can start to learn what examiners want from you by familiarising yourself with a few common question keywords, and the circumstances in which they are used.

Understand the "command words"

Your teacher or tutor will hopefully have discussed these with you, as every subject has slightly different expectations. But here are some general principles that will apply in most cases to get you started.

WHAT questions are usually straightforward questions where you are being asked to jot down some standard points from the syllabus, often in exchange for a relatively modest number of marks.

EXPLAIN / HOW questions generally want a process from you. How to make iron in a blast furnace, or how the shooting of Archduke Franz Ferdinand led to the outbreak of the First World War, for example. Take the examiner logically through the answer, one step at a time. If you're not clear on all the steps in the process before you start writing, scribble out quick notes on rough paper and try to work out what you're missing.

EVALUATE / ASSESS questions usually involve two or more viewpoints, positions, or opinions. It's your job to argue for the first position, then argue for the second position, and then summarise why you think one of these is true, and why.

Check the number of marks available for a rough indication of how many points to put down: for a four-mark question, you might aim for two points in favour of each position, and a statement summarising which position you come down in favour of.

DISCUSS questions are put in to test what you know about an issue: these are typically longer questions, with a good number of marks up for grabs. "Discuss" questions often give you more freedom to be expansive, and really show off your knowledge of the topic. You might want to consider jotting down a mini-plan if a reasonably high-mark "discuss" question has popped up in a short answer section of a paper.

What / Why / How MIGHT questions usually indicate having to do a wee bit of thinking. The question is flagging up that what you're facing here will require a little more than just standard bookwork. The answer can't be copied verbatim from the syllabus, you'll need to apply what you know to an unfamiliar situation and work out what you think is going on.

EVALUATE THE EXTENT TO WHICH questions are more commonly seen in arts subjects. They are similar to "Evaluate" questions, and should be approached in a similar way, only this time you might want to caveat your answer rather than coming down firmly in favour of one point of view or position.

SHOW THAT / PROVE THAT questions are usually found in calculation-based papers such as Physics or Maths. They expect you to reach a final answer which is provided in the question. These questions are ones to look forward to, because if you can get back to the answer the question is looking for, you can be reasonably certain your answer is correct.

Interpreting the other clues the examiner leaves

The layout of an exam paper or the wording of its questions can often give you clues as to how you should answer them.

Most of the time, these clues are helpful – but not always!

Information given
In the majority of cases, all of the information given in the question is necessary to answer the question.

If you're given a set of numbers for a calculation in science, or a glossary of words for a language translation, tick them off as you use them. If there's a word or term you haven't used, ask yourself why not – have you missed something?

There are occasional times where examiners may give you extra information that isn't relevant. In such cases, they are probably testing your ability to sift out superfluous data and the right answer may require you to ignore some of the information provided.

If in doubt, stick to what you know.

Space allocated
Write as much as you think you need to write to fully answer the question, but don't ramble on unnecessarily. The space allowed for your answer gives you a rough guide as to how much the examiner expects you to write, but remember that handwriting styles and sizes vary wildly, and some people write more concisely than others.

Space allocated is only a rough guide: if you're confident you have done all you can to win the marks and double-checked there's nothing else you could add, don't write a load of waffle just to fill the space.

23. WALK THE WALK

"Everyone shines, given the right lighting."

– Susan Cain, author

Another good way to make the examiner happy is by making your answer paper look great.

Aim to write answers that look like those written by a top student, who *knows* exactly what they are doing, even if you don't *feel* like you know exactly what you're doing.

A well-presented paper has three main benefits:

- We subconsciously grow into the image we portray to the world. So if your paper looks scrappy, you'll be more likely to have messy thoughts; but if your paper is neat and orderly (even if not every answer is right), you'll be more likely to be thinking clearly too.

- A neatly laid-out paper helps you to work more accurately, avoiding mistakes by getting things muddled or lost. You'll also find it much easier to check your workings for errors later (see Step 30).

- As soon as the examiner looks at your paper, they will immediately start to judge your work based on its appearance. They will try and be fair and objective, of course, but they can't help an initial bias. If it looks like a paper written by a strong candidate, they'll be in a mark-giving frame of mind. If your working is all over the place, and you're making them dig through to figure out what marks are worth awarding to you, you may find the marks being awarded less freely.

Examiners are hugely rushed when they review papers – don't make them work to find the evidence that you are a top student. Make your exam paper *look* like it was written by a top student, and even if an answer isn't perfect, you may score a higher mark for it if it's a well-presented response.

Sort your handwriting out

You wouldn't write your exam papers in invisible ink, so don't write them in illegible writing. A clear, joined-up hand gives a great first impression to the examiner.

Most people write too small: try an exercise to learn how to get this right.

Take a short, simple sentence (if you're stuck for inspiration, try the typographer's classic, "the quick brown fox jumped over the lazy dog"), and write it four times on a piece of normal lined paper. The first time, write it in a size slightly smaller than your normal handwriting. Second time round, use your normal handwriting size. Third time, increase the size of your handwriting – make the letters larger, and include more space between words. Fourth time, make it comically large – but still within the lines of the ruled paper.

Then ask around a few friends, maybe even your teacher, to find out which version they prefer. Which is easiest to read? Which looks neatest?

You might find the answer is the third or even fourth versions of your chosen sentence. If so, try and adopt this new writing style from now on. You'll need a bit of practice to make this your new default; make sure some of this practice is under timed conditions.

Signpost and structure your writing

For longer, "essay-style" questions, use clear language to signpost where you are in an argument. Let me show you what I mean, using an "evaluate" or "discuss whether" type question as an example:

"There are three reasons to believe [xxx] is true, and three reasons to believe [xxx] is untrue. It could be argued that [xxx] is true; first, because [point 1]. Second, because [point 2]. And third, because [point 3]. On the other hand, it could be argued that [xxx] is untrue; first, because [point 1]. Second, because [point 2]. And third, because [point 3]. In conclusion, [zzz]".

This example demonstrates a number of useful principles:

- Use numbers "first, second, third" to number and signpost your points as you make them.

- Use connecting words to indicate where you are in your argument.

- In this case, you're arguing for and against something, so the structure "on the one hand... / on the other..." works well.

- For a shorter argument, a simple "however" might be enough to indicate when you're switching from points in favour to points against.

- If you're simply listing points in favour, you could use words like "moreover" or "furthermore" to show when you're moving into a new section.

- "Therefore" or "hence" are good words to use when one point logically leads to the next.

• Have a clear introduction, in which you set out the structure you'll be adopting ("three points for, three points against" in this case), and end with a strong conclusion, which summarises your argument, referring back to the original question to make sure you've answered it fully. Some students like to write their conclusion first so they know where they are going with their argument.

If you're explaining the steps in a process, do so really clearly. For some non-language papers (e.g. in science), it might be fine to number your points down the side of the page ("1, 2, 3"), starting each step in the process on a new numbered line; otherwise, you can do this in writing ("first, second, third").

Good structure not only makes it much clearer where you're making the points that should earn you marks, but also improves the overall quality of your writing, which could be worth marks in its own right.

Set out calculations and workings clearly

Good structure doesn't just apply to prose or essay-style answers, it also pays to set out calculations clearly.

The following steps are a good starting point for solving problems. Show each of these steps on a separate line:

1. Starting by writing out the formula

2. Substituting known values

3. Rearranging if necessary

4. Doing the calculation

5. Writing the answer clearly, with the relevant unit

Being rigorous in this way not only makes your answer easier for the examiner to mark (and for you to check), it also helps you pick up "method" marks for earlier steps in the calculation even if you got the final answer wrong.

A few further tips for laying out your workings:

- Don't do too much work in one step: break it up into separate components, and tackle each in turn. I was always taught to work out "Mr" on a separate line in

Chemistry, for example. This reduces the risk of you making a mistake, even if you think the calculation is easy, and again, helps pick up intermediate marks even if you get the final answer wrong.

- Use a ruler for straight lines in diagrams and charts, and when drawing graphs, be precise in the positioning of points and lines so they are exactly where they should be.

- For calculations, keep everything vertically aligned. The "=" signs should all line up, one below the other, rather than darting round the page, with terms moving from one side to the other as needed. Keep equivalent terms vertically aligned as well, if you can: when substituting numbers into a formula, for example, put the number on Line 2 directly below the corresponding symbol on Line 1.

- Underline your final answer with a ruler, and don't forget the unit.

Check the question to make sure you've answered it: sometimes a numerical answer is insufficient, and you need to add a conclusion or recommendation in words to fully address what is asked of you.

Correcting your work

Finally, you may need to correct or add to your work. Some advance thought here can make it much easier to do this neatly:

- Consider using double-line spacing when doing language translations to insert or amend words easily.

- Leave two or three lines at the bottom of each page: if you later think of a key point you should have included, an extra line of argument you want to add, or a better explanation to include, you can use the space at the bottom of the page to add what you want to say by means of a numbered footnote or an asterisk.

- Leave a half-page or so between essays, so that you can add longer points as a numbered end-note[19], or build on your conclusion later if you think there's something missing.

- If you do make a mess of things, and you end up with a hideous web of crossing-out and scribbling, you might want to consider coming back at the end, if you have spare time, to put a line through it and write it up neatly below.

If you've planned well, the footnotes should be less frequently needed, but it's useful to know you can include them neatly if you do have to.

Make sure you get credit for all your work

Some answer sheets need your name on every section or your candidate number on every page. You might be allowed to get

---

[19] Like this, yeah?

this sort of admin done while you're waiting for the exam to start for a "marginal gain" of time.

Otherwise, and if you're running super-short of time in the exam, you could leave naming your work until after the exam has finished. You might get a few frosty glares from the invigilator if you're still writing your name on your pages after they've called time on the exam, but they'll let you finish.

After papers have been marked by an examiner, there is usually a process of "moderation", where examiners come together and check they have all been applying the same criteria to judge the work.

At these meetings, your script can sometimes – almost literally – be thrown around the table. If you've used separate answer sheets, it might be worth putting a page number at the top of each to minimise the risk that they get separated (though be sure not to write in any parts of the page you've been told not to).

After all your hard work, you want to make sure you claim all the credit you deserve for your exam paper!

24. TIME MANAGEMENT MASTERY

"How did it get so late so soon?"

– Dr. Seuss

The caveat "provided you have time" has come up quite a few times already in the context of the exam techniques we've been discussing, so it's high time we talked about the critical issue of exam timekeeping and pacing in more detail. Getting your timings wrong is one of the biggest reasons for exam disappointments.

What should you do about it?

Keep an eye on the clock

The exam clock is your compass, your North Star, your lighthouse. Keep on top of it, and don't let it play tricks on you.

You'll usually see an official exam clock, and a board noting the exam start and finish time.

Your exams won't often start on the hour, more commonly a couple of minutes either way. Your brain has a habit of rounding times up or down to the nearest hour, such that 1057 and 1103 are both "basically 1100" in your head: but when it comes down to the final ten minutes of the paper, that really makes a difference. It's funny – a finish time of 1057 can feel like three minutes stolen; a finish of 1103 can feel like three minutes bonus time.

Keep an eye on that clock. I'd suggest checking in at least every ten minutes or so, to make sure you are on track.

Make a glance at the clock like looking in your rear-view mirror (if you drive): a second-nature habit that operates almost outside of the main focus of your attention. You want to feel as if 98% of your attention is on answering the question in front of you, but 2% is reserved to be your timings supervisor, keeping you moving through the paper at the right pace.

Give this inner "timings supervisor" the authority to moderate the pace at which you're working: that may mean you need to speed up and sacrifice a little detail to avoid getting behind.

Deviating from your gameplan

If you've got your exam gameplan figured out (Step 3), you should know what "on track" means in terms of the times you should be hitting various milestones through the paper, or how long you've got for each question.

In general, you should be disciplined with your timings: you optimised the plan to serve you best, and deviating from it may mean you won't score as highly. A few minutes either way usually won't make much difference – you could normally spend an extra five minutes on a section without throwing your overall schedule off too much, provided you have a plan where you'll make the time up.

But even the best-designed gameplan in the world can't account for the uncertain circumstances you might find yourself in on exam day. So feel free to apply your judgement in the moment, and make more substantial changes to the gameplan if you have to.

The litmus test question to ask yourself is: will changing the gameplan give me a better chance of getting more marks? If the answer is "yes", then do it. For example:

- Running out of time to check your work through? More often than not, it will be better to invest that time in finishing all of the questions, rather than leaving questions unanswered and going back to check ones you've already completed.

- Have lots to say on one essay, but really struggling to remember relevant material for the second one? You might pick up more marks overall by reallocating a few minutes from the weaker one to the stronger one, and using that extra time to bust out a really great essay on your stronger topic.

- Are you feeling particularly flustered? It may serve you well to get some marks under your belt and regain your momentum. Flick through the paper until you find a question that looks do-able, and tackle that next. You should soon be feeling calmer.

Keep your wits about you, use your common sense, and remember the golden rule: what's going to get me more marks?

Running short on time

If your clock-glancing and work-pacing goes well, you should avoid running out of time on papers. Prevention is far better than a cure: the earlier you can spot your timings drifting and take action to pull yourself back on track, the better. You may have wanted 45 minutes per essay, but if there's only an hour left on the clock, much better to write two half-hour essays than a 45-minute essay and a 15-minute essay.

If you find yourself with a more serious time problem, here's what to do about it.

If you're trying to finish shorter answer questions, aim to make it to the end of the paper, even if that means writing less detailed answers. The first half of a question is often easier than the second half, so it might be best to leave a question half-finished and move on to a fresh one, where you can pick up the easy marks much more rapidly.

A little tip: if the questions are grouped into multi-part questions (e.g. 8a, 8b, 8c), you'll often find part "a" is very straightforward, particularly early on in the paper. In the final minutes of the exam, make sure you've grabbed all the "low hanging fruit" you can find first, to scoop up as many easy marks as you can in the time available.

What if you're behind on an essay paper?

Your first option is to simply be less detailed: ramp up the pace at which you're scribbling down the main points, prioritising the information which is essential to your argument.

If that's still too much of a stretch, you could switch to note form, and jot down as much of the remainder of your argument and supporting facts as you can, perhaps using bullet points, to indicate to the examiner what you wanted to say. Leave a note in the margin to explain you ran out of time. You should hopefully pick up at least some credit for your ideas and knowledge.

As a last resort, you could always direct the examiner to your essay plan, to show where you intended to go with an essay you haven't had time to write. Don't expect a great mark, but it could be better than nothing.

25. MAXIMISING MEMORY RECALL

"It's not what you know…"

– From the proverb "it's not what you know, it's who you know."

By and large, I think there's plenty of truth in that proverb, though not when it comes to exams.

Exams are almost entirely about testing "what you know"!

If you've done your studying well[20], you'll have a lot of relevant information in your memory, but occasionally, it will feel like you just can't seem to pull out that piece of data you need when you're sitting in the exam hall.

So what to do when you find yourself struggling for that crucial fact, figure or formula? Here's my four-step process for digging deeper into your memory than you ever thought possible.

Step 1. Check your mnemonics

Did you have any mnemonics (e.g. rhymes or acronyms) or other memory tricks you planned to use to help you remember the information? Even if you thought "I'll never use that", were there any mnemonics you heard your teacher / lecturer /

---

[20] Download my Exam Success Cheat Sheet at examstudyexpert.com/outsmart-bonuses for the time-saving, mark-maximising secrets you probably haven't heard before.

friends using? Spend a moment trying to resurrect the mnemonic from memory – it might be a great route in to recalling the information itself.

Step 2. Visualise

Close your eyes, put your head in your hands, and picture yourself when you were learning that information. Where were you – a revision room, your classroom? How did you learn the information – can you picture it on the board, can you remember muttering it under your breath? Breathe deeply a few times, relax, and focus: the answer will often present itself.

Step 3. Warm up your memory network

Nothing yet? Let's go deeper.

The parts of the brain that store memories are often described as networks of interlinked nodes. When you think about a piece of information, you "activate" the node that represents that piece of information: but not only that, nodes that represent *related* pieces of information also start to get excited[21]. The related information is not yet "fully activated", but is certainly "warmed up".

You will therefore find it easier to recall the fact you need if you have related pieces of information bubbling away in your mind.

---

[21] OK, this is a simplification: look up "spreading activation theory of memory" if you want the theoretical background.

If I mention "1066" to a Brit and ask them to name a famous historical figure, they're much more likely to say "William the Conqueror" than if I'd mentioned any other historical date at random. Or if I said "July 4th" to an American, they would be much more likely than normal to name a founding father[22] as a historical figure.

You can use this principle to your advantage: try jotting down a few related facts, or simply "think around" the fact itself, bringing to mind as much supporting and associated information as you can, circling in on the thing you are actually trying to remember. If I've forgotten the name of a historical figure, for instance, I might think about what I know about that person's activities and achievements, or about other historical names s/he was associated with.

Step 4. Cut your losses – for now

Still nothing? Time to move on: you need to keep moving through the paper to avoid your timings slipping.

It's sometimes good practice to put something plausible down, even if you're almost certain it's wrong. Just sometimes, once in a while, you'll be right! I wouldn't deliberately drop incorrect facts into an essay, though – it may drag down the score for the

---

[22] And for similar reasons, a reader of this book is more likely than normal to have named Benjamin Franklin as the first founding father that came to mind, given that we mentioned him earlier.

whole essay if you're mixing accurate and inaccurate information. Perhaps best to leave that detail out.

Either way, leave plenty of space to come back and write a different answer in later. You'll be amazed at the number of times the answer will spring to mind when you're working on a completely unrelated part of the exam, and you can go back and fill in that blank you left for yourself, no doubt with some satisfaction.

26. THE SECRETS TO MULTIPLE-CHOICE QUESTIONS

"Your life is not a simulation; it's the real game. Play wisely."

– Richelle Goodrich, author

Many students like the idea of a multiple-choice paper: how hard can it be if one of the right answers is already in front of you?

Well, sometimes, pretty hard! Examiners can be tricksy, slipping in answer options which are so very nearly right to tempt you, to check just how rigorously you really know your stuff.

Read carefully

To outsmart a multiple-choice exam, start by reading the question carefully: follow the "ninja question-reading" method from Step 20 to make sure you don't miss a trick.

Then read EVERY answer slowly – don't jump to circle the first one you see that looks right. Just because an answer sounds right, it doesn't mean it is, and when you read the others, you might realise it was a decoy "nearly but not quite right" option.

Consider each answer in turn. As with choosing questions, I use a clear scoring method to rate how good each option seems:

- ✓✓ – definitely correct (but still read the other options just to be sure!)

- ✓ – pretty sure this is correct

- ✓? – may be correct, but not very sure

- x? – probably wrong, but not very sure

- xx – definitely wrong

You can be pretty confident of what the right answer is when you see only one ticked option, the rest with crosses beside them.

There's a UK quiz show called *Eggheads* which features super-high achieving quiz takers with vast general knowledge. When answering a multiple-choice question, an "Egghead" quizzer would very often say "well it's not A because ___, and it's not C because___, so it must be B. And I happen to know B is right because ___".

In other words, they don't just confirm the right answer, they eliminate the wrong ones as well. Aim to do the same thing when you're tackling multiple-choice questions.

If you're not sure, hopefully the scoring has at least narrowed down the number of possible options. Sometimes, examiners will be devious and throw you two or more options that would earn a tick from you. Look deeper into the subtleties of the wording – one will be more correct or precise than the other "distractor" option. If you had been barrelling through the questions at maximum speed, you might have put down the distractor as being the right answer – but by slowing down and taking a more considered approach, you've avoided the trap.

Multiple guess?

Know whether the paper is negatively or positively marked: in other words, will you lose marks for incorrect answers, or are you simply awarded marks for each right answer?

If the paper is positively marked – i.e. you won't lose marks for wrong answers – then never, ever leave a question blank. Guess if you have to. You've got a one in four chance of picking up the mark (assuming there are four answer options).

If you're really stuck, here are a few tricks that are better than taking a wild guess:

- Sometimes the least jargon-y answer is the right one.

- Look out for a grammatical match in "complete the sentence" – sometimes only one of the answer options can be right because it's the only one that makes a linguistically accurate sentence.

- Which answer "feels" the most familiar? Often your gut is right.

If all else fails, when you're doing a positively marked multiple-choice exam, always, always guess – you have nothing to lose, and potentially, a mark to gain!

Should I guess even if it's negatively marked?

Negative marking, where you are docked a mark for a wrong answer, is an indication that the examiners are trying to discourage wild guesses. So should you still guess? Things get a little trickier here, but fortunately, we can call on some scientific research on the benefits of guessing in negatively marked multiple-choice papers.

- **You think you know:** if you feel you're making an "educated guess" – you know a bit about the question but aren't certain – the science says you should go for it. It seems students are right much more often than they're wrong under these circumstances.

- **You have no idea:** what about a totally wild guess? Intriguingly, the evidence *still* says you should make the guess, and you'll be right slightly more often than you're wrong. Presumably, there is something rattling round in the dark, dusty depths of your mind on enough of these wild guesses to point you in the right direction at least some of the time.

But the margin for success on the wild guesses is pretty finely balanced, and whether you come out ahead will depend on a number of factors, including how strong a student you are. Personally, I would play it safe, and would suggest that on the negatively marked papers you:

- Do make educated guesses, but;

- Don't make wild guesses, unless you're a confident student and feel you know the topic really well.

Pacing yourself

Your gameplan for multiple-choice papers should be focused on question-answering rate. Divide the minutes available by the number of questions to figure out how many minutes you have per question.

Pace yourself accordingly, with regular clock-glancing to regulate the speed at which you're working through the paper, and keep you on track.

For example, a one-hour paper with 50 questions works out at a minute per question with ten minutes checking time at the end – pretty comfortable. After fifteen minutes, if you're somewhere around Question 15 then you're doing just fine, but if you're on Question 10 you'll need to pick up the pace a little, and if you're on Question 20 you can afford to go more carefully.

If the time constraints are quite severe, it may be a good idea to circle trickier questions to come back to at the end. Put your best guess down for now, but make a note to come back to that question at the end if you have time. Again, unless the paper is negatively marked, make sure you put an answer down for every question.

27. The Power of Perseverance

"There are no traffic jams on the extra mile."

– Zig Ziglar, ace salesman

A big exam sitting can be a real test of physical and mental stamina.

But where there's adversity, there's opportunity for you to give yourself an advantage by going the extra mile.

Sheer diligence

This is less true on higher-level university and college courses when you're surrounded by highly motivated colleagues, but certainly in exams through middle-school and high-school, you'll find that many of your peers will hit a wall with around fifteen minutes remaining.

They figure that, with the bulk of the exam paper attempted and the majority of time on the clock gone, the day is already won or lost. They are either satisfied what they've done is "already good enough", or they despair that it "will never be good enough"; either way, losing drive, and producing very little additional work in the remaining time.

If you remain diligent and focused right to the final minute, you can unlock a realm of marks inaccessible to your colleagues who don't persevere as long as you do.

The nice thing about this is that it's true for students at all levels.

Say you tend to perform about the middle of your class, and you're facing a two-hour paper. Everyone works hard for the first 90 minutes: you might expect to score an average number of marks during that time. But in the final half-hour, when everyone else starts to check out, you stay focused and productive. You'll continue to earn marks at a steady rate, closing the gap on some of your classmates who normally perform higher, and maybe even giving you a shot at outperforming them.

This is especially true for papers that require producing a large volume of written material, like English.

Physical stamina

It's very common for your hand to hurt in the middle of a long writing paper.

To put your mind at rest, it's very unlikely that your hand will give you so much discomfort that it distracts you from fulfilling your potential – you'll be able to keep going, but it won't be very nice at the time!

But a little preparation can make your life in the exam room that much more comfortable.

First, pen choice: make sure you have a pen that is comfortable to hold, and dispenses ink freely onto the page with minimal pressure. Some stationery shops will let you try out a whole range of pens before you find one that's good for you – though you can never really know you've found a winner until you get it home and do some serious writing with it. Once you have been working with a good pen for a few days and are happy, go out and buy a lot of them to see you through revision and exam time.

Then think about how you hold the pen. Your grip should be assured but gentle – don't grip tightly. Get your forearm and shoulder involved in creating a fluid writing motion, don't just leave it all to the wrist.

Finally, if you've got some time left before your exams, make sure you've got plenty of practice in writing rapidly with a pen for extended periods of time – don't just do all your studying on a laptop.

If your hand starts to get sore in the exam, shake it out, check your grip isn't too tight, and battle on.

Mental stamina

If you've got a shorter paper and the adrenaline is pumping, you'll probably have all the energy you need to keep working through a full paper.

But some of my exam success coaching clients face seriously long papers. Three hours was standard in my own student days; I've had recent conversations with students facing four-hour testing marathons.

When exams get this long, you may well start to flag as the exam drags on.

Here are a few tips to get you through, and keep those energy levels up:

- Stay hydrated: take on board water through the exam. Just don't go at it too hard too early and end up needing too many bathroom breaks.

- Avoid caffeine (if you can): it might be tempting to load up on coffee before a big paper – but be careful. It might keep you alert early on in the paper, but you risk a "caffeine crash" later on. So if you're an occasional or light caffeine consumer, I'd try to avoid it altogether on exam day. (More on this in Step 5).

- Don't be afraid to take a mini-break (see Step 17), especially between questions and sections. Just pause in your seat, perhaps have a little water, think about how you'll celebrate when it's all over, then get back to work and go at it again.

- Fit for exams: long-term, one of the best things you can do for permanently raised energy levels is to be physically fit, via regular exercise.

28. SURVIVING TOUGH QUESTIONS

"I'm not telling you it is going to be easy — I'm telling you it's going to be worth it."

– Art Williams, insurance billionaire

Exams are often designed with a spectrum of questions to cater to students of all abilities. There may be some really straightforward ones that even the lowest-performing student can handle, right through to a few brain teasers that are designed to separate the student that gets 90% from the one that gets 95%.

How you deal with the tougher questions on the exam will really separate you from the herd.

Practical tactics to get past difficult questions

There are a few strategies you can deploy to see you through unexpectedly challenging questions.

- For numerical problems in Sciences and Maths, start by writing down all the information the question contains. That might be a list of terms. Check the formula booklet, your cheat-sheet or your memory for a formula that relates some or all of the terms you've just written down. Maybe you can do an intermediate calculation that gets you part of the way, even if you don't know where to go from there –

that might score you some marks by itself, and sometimes, may make the rest of the solution clear.

- For language questions: stop trying to answer it all in one go, and break it down. Write down what you *do* know, if anything. Trying to translate a long sentence you only know half of? Write out the sentence, with the translations you do know underneath. If you're not sure, write down two or more options for the word. Can you use the "memory mining" techniques or simply common-sense based "guesswork" to fill in the blanks? A plausible guess is always better than leaving white space.

- Can you work backwards from an answer you know or believe to be true?

- Can you make a guess at an early stage in a question, to allow you to pick up "error carried forward" marks for later steps you can do?

- Often, the tougher questions in papers are when the examiner asks you to apply what you do know to unfamiliar situations. Start by writing down what you understand of the basics on the subject or issue – even just a definition of a key term. You might even get some marks for that. Don't let the unfamiliar scenario put you off: go back to the principles or rules you know, and apply brainpower carefully and methodically, to see if you can come up with a plausible solution.

- Just sometimes, what you have learned on your course can be a barrier to you getting the answer right. Step back and ask yourself what you might have made of this question two years ago, just based on common sense, without any knowledge of the course.

An example of the last one in action, taken from a real Science paper sat by UK 16-year-olds: "suggest why inventors used a mixture of copper and silver". Only 10% got the mark – and it wasn't awarded for knowing about the physical properties of these metals (e.g. they both conduct electricity); no, it was for stating that pure silver would have been too expensive!

The moral of the story: if a question makes you go "huh?" write down some aspect of the topic that seems relevant, *and* step back to think whether there are any unusual / left-field deductions the examiner might expect you to make.

It's about going the extra mile again, and being greedy for any marks you can pick up: many students will be too intimidated by a hard-looking question to even attempt it, but if you can get some relevant information down, like an opening definition of a key term, or a formula, you may at least unlock the first couple of marks.

Remember, if you're finding a question tough, or even finding a whole paper tough, chances are most other candidates are too. Grade boundaries are not fixed: a paper that everyone found difficult will have a lower-than-usual grade boundary. By persevering through adversity, and scrabbling to pick up marks where you can, you'll give yourself the best shot at clearing the grade boundary, wherever it is set.

Let other students give up: strive to push through, do what you can, and give yourself the best possible chance of success.

Judging when to move on

Don't let a tough question derail you for too long – it's a mistake to sweat for so long over one question that you have to rush mark-rich questions you can answer later. Know when to cut your losses.

This "give up and come back to it" advice is commonly given by teachers, and for good reason: it helps you keep your overall exam timings on track, making sure you pick up the marks you deserve later in the paper.

But you're also giving yourself a better chance of figuring out the answer by walking away from the question and coming back with fresh eyes later. While you're working on the rest of the paper, your brain will tick away on the problem in the background, without you even noticing – and it might be starting to develop a viable solution. If any flashes of inspiration pop into your mind for the tough question when you're working on a different part of the paper, be sure to jot them down.

There's a balance to moving on too quickly from a tough question, though: if you think you're close to unlocking the question, an extra few minutes may be time well spent. Any time you switch task, there is a "switching cost" involved, the time your brain needs to move from one problem to another.

So, if you're deep in a question and you feel you're making progress solving it, it might be worth staying immersed now to save yourself the time cost of getting back up to speed with it later.

29. Dealing With The Unexpected

Frodo: "I wish none of this had happened."

Gandalf: "So do all who live to see such times, but that is not for them to decide. All we have to decide is what to do with the time that is given to us."

– J.R.R. Tolkien, The Lord of the Rings

Sometimes an exam can throw real curveballs in your face, more so than just your typical tough question or two.

Depending on how bad things look, this may take some courage to work through, but hold your nerve, and persevere.

Mistakes on the paper

Mistakes happen.

I once had an announcement in the middle of a university Chemistry exam: "could I have your attention? A mistake has been identified on the paper." We were given some extra time to allow for the error.

If it's a national public exam, it's very unlikely that there will be errors in the paper – they are subjected to intense scrutiny – but they do happen very occasionally, and you're unlikely to get a correction notice while you're still taking the exam.

If you think you've spotted a mistake, raise the issue with the invigilator. There might not be much the invigilator can do about it: if there is no correction issued, then it's vital you answer the question as it is written, to the best of your ability, rather than the question you *think* they meant to ask. Trying to second-guess the examiner is a risky strategy – after all, there's a chance that you could have been wrong about there being a mistake in the paper.

Mistakes on the exam are generally no cause for concern: if there is one, it is the examiner's burden to bear, often by discarding that question from being marked entirely. Not your problem.

I don't remember learning this…?

What if you're faced with questions about unexpected topics, or simply questions so downright odd you can't make head or tail of them?

If there are just a few marks at stake on one of these odd or unexpected questions, give it your best shot, and move on. Perhaps add it to your list of questions to revisit at the end if you have time, but don't get too worked up about it.

But what if it's a much larger section of the exam? Say, for example, you're choosing an essay, and can't see any titles that relate to options or modules you studied during the year. You'll reread the list of questions in disbelief: how can there not be *any* questions that you can write on?

It can be a frightening feeling when a major upset like that happens on a paper you've been working hard for all year. Take a moment to have a sip of water, breathe, then double-check the list of questions, carefully, one at a time. Perhaps you missed something – was one of them actually about your topic, but worded unusually, or approaching it in a novel or tangential way?

Spare a brief moment's thought in the exam to possible resolutions: if you don't think it's your fault that you've ended up in this position, you've probably got strong grounds on which to appeal. The examiners might discount the offending question from your overall mark, or even offer a resit.

In the meantime, your job is to make the best of a bad situation – pick one of the questions that gives you the best chance of cobbling something coherent together, and write up some form of answer based on your general knowledge, and perhaps knowledge from other parts of the course that could be pressed into service as being relevant to this question.

Adverse circumstances

Finally, there may be times when circumstances beyond your control transpire against you, to present a significant barrier to you performing well on exam day.

Some exam boards will make special allowances by way of extra marks for issues like ill-health or serious distractions in the exam.

By way of example, I've summarised some of the "special circumstances" from the main exam council in the UK, which is in charge of overseeing most major school exams, including GCSEs and A-Levels:

% Extra Marks Allowed	Examples of circumstances
4-5%: maximum allowance for exceptional cases	• Terminal illness of parent / carer • Recent bereavement of close family member • Major surgery at or near time of the exam
2-3%: more common categories	• Recent traumatic experience (e.g. death of friend) • Recent serious illness or broken limbs
1%: minor problems	• Ongoing noise distraction on the day • Stress or anxiety for which medication is prescribed • Minor upset arising from administrative problems • Hay fever on the day of an exam

NB: This is provided for illustrative purposes only, and is simplified from the source[23]. Always seek guidance from your school exams officer or your tutors if you think special circumstances might apply to you.

---

[23] https://www.jcq.org.uk/exams-office/access-arrangements-and-special-consideration/regulations-and-guidance/a-guide-to-the-special-consideration-process-2018-2019

The purpose of allowances such as these is to give all exam candidates a fair chance. Don't see this as a system to be exploited to give you maximum marks: if you plead a special case over a borderline issue this year, you may use up some goodwill and have a more serious problem in future taken less seriously.

But if you were significantly disadvantaged by circumstances on the day of the exam, there may be something that can be done.

30. Final Chance For Marks: Checking

"You have ten minutes left."

– Your invigilator again

Nearly made it to the end!

You've got every question answered, but you're not out of the woods yet – you've still got precious minutes of exam time left. Use every moment available to you to go the extra mile, to check your work, edit it, correct errors, and generally squeeze every last mark you possibly can out of your paper.

In the process of planning your exam gameplan (Step 3), you will have figured out whether you should leave time for checking, and if so, how much.

Not every gameplan will have planned in dedicated time for checking – but if you run ahead of time and finish early, you use every spare moment you have to check anyway, regardless of whether you intended to or not.

Here are some top tips on squeezing out every available mark through checking well.

The checker's checklist

Some things you might want to look out for when you're checking your work:

- Have you answered the question that was asked (rather than the question you thought was asked)?

- Have you been precise in use of technical terminology?

- Are there any points you've missed, or extra facts you could drop in to pep up your answer? You've left space at the bottom of the page / at the end of your essay for extra footnotes / endnotes, right (see Step 23)?

- Have you been clear in your points, or do your words seem confused when you read them back? Can you do anything to clarify?

- If you're calculating numerical answers about the real world, apply some judgement and ask yourself whether your answer makes sense. A car pulling away from an inner-city junction at 300mph or a man weighing 2 kilos (4 pounds) should raise your eyebrow!

- Have you included a unit at the end of a calculation? Is it the right one: does it match the sort of answer the question was looking for?

- Have you used all the information the examiner gave you? If not, do you have a strong reason for not doing so?

- Elegant language: if you are being marked on your use of language, are there any boring words or clunky phrases you can upgrade?

- Have you been accurate in your spelling and grammar, especially for language papers where the accuracy of your writing carries more weight?

A tip for written language answers, where accuracy matters, is to split the checking process up into separate stages. Check three or four times, and focus on something different each time: for example, on your first check, you're looking out for verb endings, on your second check, you're focusing on the gender of nouns and adjectives (masculine / feminine), and so on. It may be easier than trying to check for everything all in the same step.

It's sometimes easier to spot spelling mistakes by reading your answer backwards, starting with the very last word you've written, and working through to the first, checking each word in turn.

It may sound obvious, but have you read all the pages of the exam paper? Check to see whether there is a back page you've missed, or whether you've turned two pages at once, particularly if you've finished surprisingly early.

Never leave an exam early

I don't care if everyone else left half an hour ago and you are the only one left.

I don't care if you found the paper a doddle, or whether it was the worst thing ever.

I don't care if it's your last paper and it's the most gorgeously sunny day outside.

Stay until the bitter end, double-checking, augmenting, fixing and annotating until you have no more time. Even if that extra fifteen minutes of checking only helps you squeeze one extra mark out of the paper, it's worth it.

It could be that single mark is what stands between you and the grade of your dreams.

So use every second, and be ruthless in seeking out where you could pick up that precious extra point.

31. Stop, Reset, And Go Again

"Stop writing now, the exam is over. Stay seated until an invigilator has collected your exam paper."

– Your invigilator one last time

Made it! There is nothing more you can do now.

Check, name and leave

Double-check that:

- Your personal information is properly marked up

- Any pages you need to number have been numbered

- You have put a tag through any spare answer sheets if that's what you're supposed to do

- You have separated out any rough paper, whether you have written on it or not

You're usually not allowed to take rough paper out of the exam hall – apparently, it's so you don't sneak blank sheets of exam-hall style rough paper out of the hall, only to bring them back in with notes on for another exam.

Gather your belongings from the back of the exam hall, and step out of exam land back into reality.

Outside the exam hall

Chat to your friends, but keep it brief, and avoid talking about specifics. You can't go back and change your answers now: you will only spook each other out by discussing what you should have said.

I remember immediately after the first major exam I ever sat (GCSE Maths), some of my classmates started dissecting a couple of tough questions. I'd come out with a different answer to them, so we spent a good hour debating it, eventually finding an empty classroom, and thrashing it out on the whiteboard.

Turns out, I'd almost certainly got the answer wrong. As you can imagine, that wasn't a very nice thing to discover.

Good use of my time? I think not.

At best, you might conclude that you got some answers right, but that knowledge doesn't carry much practical benefit now. At worst, you might decide – rightly or wrongly – that you made a mistake, which could knock your confidence ahead of tomorrow's exams.

As you walk out of the exam hall, the exam you've just taken should immediately fall down your list of life priorities, from being the most important thing in your life to the least important.

Taking its place as your new top priority is the next exam, awaiting you this afternoon, tomorrow, or the day after.

Pausing for breath

If your next paper is later the same day, you don't have much chance to catch your breath. Perhaps an hour or two in which to look over your final condensed notes for that exam, and eat a good lunch (might be worth preparing food the night before for double-exam days).

More often, you should have at least a little time before your next paper, even if it's just an afternoon. How best to use the time?

When you come out of an exam, you'll naturally want to chill out for a bit. You've earned yourself a leisurely lunch, and maybe an episode or two of whatever TV show you're into at the moment. Something that you find funny, or calming and relaxing, or that lets you escape to your fantasy land / universe of choice for a bit. Or you might prefer to bury your head in a great book for an hour, catch up with friends, or play some sport.

Aim to take a quality hour or two out, ideally not much more, unless you've just survived a particularly brutal paper, and need a little longer than normal to recover. Then when you're ready, head back to your desk to do your final prep (Step 10) for the next paper, and get ready to do it all again.

EPILOGUE: WHEN IT'S ALL OVER

"It always seems impossible until it is done."

– Nelson Mandela

Then all of a sudden, you'll be facing your final exam.

It can seem a lifetime away before you start taking exams, but the day of your last paper will come around quicker than you think once you've taken your first.

It's a memorable day when you close your coursebooks for good, and set out for the exam hall one last time.

The rush of anticipation when you turn the page, look inside your last exam paper and set to work on the questions inside.

That bubble of satisfaction rising in your throat as you put down your pen for the last time, shake out your aching hand, turn your exam script in to the invigilator and step out into the sunshine, into freedom.

And now, at last, you have that blissful feeling that it's all over, with the summer months stretching luxuriously before you, and the knowledge that you are free...[24]

---

[24] ...until next year, at any rate!

* * *

My friend, I wish you every success in your exams. I'll be rooting for you.

And remember: there are no limits!

HOW TO GET IN TOUCH, AND A FINAL REQUEST...

If you enjoyed this book, why not share the love and leave us a short a review on Amazon? It doesn't have to be long – a sentence or two is more than enough to be extremely helpful for us.

Head to your local Amazon store:

- For UK, see
https://www.amazon.co.uk/dp/B07DM8K58B

- For US and rest of world, click
https://www.amazon.com/dp/B07DM8K58B

- For Australia, click
https://www.amazon.com.au/dp/B07DM8K58B

- For India, click
https://www.amazon.in/dp/B07DM8K58B#customerReviews

And scroll down to find the "write a customer review" button under the "review this product" heading.

Thank you in advance for your review, it means so much.

* * * * * *

If you have any comments or suggestions, or want to share your success story, you can reach me at examstudyexpert.com/contact.

Thank you, and once again, very best of luck with your exams!

I'll be rooting for you.

BIBLIOGRAPHY

References

The following scholarly articles underpin points made throughout this book:

Hospitals that use checklists have lower infection rates (Four Principles, Principle Two).

Haynes, A., Weiser, T., Berry, W., Lipsitz, S., Breizat, A., Dellinger, E., Herbosa, T., Joseph, S., Kibatala, P., Lapitan, M., Merry, A., Moorthy, K., Reznick, R., Taylor, B. and Gawande, A. (2009). A Surgical Safety Checklist to Reduce Morbidity and Mortality in a Global Population. *New England Journal of Medicine*, [online] 360(5), pp.491-499. Available at: https://www.nejm.org/doi/full/10.1056/NEJMsa0810119 [Accessed 4 Jun. 2019].

Pilots that use checklists fly safer planes (Four Principles, Principle Two).

Degani, A. and Wiener, E. (1993). Cockpit Checklists: Concepts, Design, and Use. *Human Factors: The Journal of the Human Factors and Ergonomics Society*, 35(2), pp.345-359.

Japanese trains or New York subway cars that are operated using checklists run with fewer delays (Four Principles, Principle Two).

Gawande, A. (2009). *The Checklist Manifesto*. New York: Metropolitan Books.

Emotion follows from physical reaction (Step 6).

Dror, O. (2013). The Cannon–Bard Thalamic Theory of Emotions: A Brief Genealogy and Reappraisal. *Emotion Review*, 6(1), pp.13-20.

Exercise is beneficial for anxiety (Step 6).

Petruzzello, S., Landers, D., Hatfield, B., Kubitz, K. and Salazar, W. (1991). A Meta-Analysis on the Anxiety-Reducing Effects of Acute and Chronic Exercise. *Sports Medicine*, 11(3), pp.143-182.

"Fear setting" – confronting your fears – inspired by the teachings of Seneca (Step 7).

Seneca (c. 65AD). "Set aside a certain number of days, during which you shall be content with the scantiest and cheapest fare, with coarse and rough dress, saying to yourself the while: 'Is this the condition that I feared?'" *Moral letters to Lucilius / Letter 18 - Wikisource, the free online library*. [online] Available at: https://en.wikisource.org/wiki/Moral_letters_to_Lucilius/Letter_18 [Accessed 4 Jun. 2019].

More recently, "fear setting" adapted and popularised by Tim Ferriss (Step 7).

Ferriss, T. (2017). *Fear-Setting: The Most Valuable Exercise I Do Every Month*. [online] The Blog of Author Tim Ferriss. Available at: https://tim.blog/2017/05/15/fear-setting/ [Accessed 4 Jun. 2019].

Some 18% of people will suffer from some kind of anxiety-related disorder every year (Step 7)

Adaa.org. (2019). Facts & Statistics | Anxiety and Depression Association of America, ADAA. [online] Available at: https://adaa.org/about-adaa/press-room/facts-statistics [Accessed 4 Jun. 2019].

The benefits of retrieval practice, or "learning by pulling information out of memory" (Step 8).

Roediger, H. and Butler, A. (2011). The critical role of retrieval practice in long-term retention. *Trends in Cognitive Sciences*, [online] 15(1), pp.20-27. Available at: http://citeseerx.ist.psu.edu/viewdoc/download?doi=10.1.1.738.2035&rep=rep1&type=pdf [Accessed 4 Jun. 2019].

The stereotype threat to academic performance of African-American students (Step 14).

Steele, C. and Aronson, J. (1995). Stereotype threat and the intellectual test performance of African Americans. *Journal of Personality and Social Psychology*, [online]

69(5), pp.797-811. Available at: http://mrnas.pbworks.com/f/claude%20steele%20stereotype%20threat%201995.pdf [Accessed 4 Jun. 2019].

The adverse effect of pressure on Scandinavian skiers (Step 18).

Krumer, Alex & Harb-Wu, Ken. (2018). Choking Under Pressure in Front of a Supportive Audience: Evidence from Professional Biathlon.

The adverse effect of pressure on Indian data-enterers (Step 18).

Ariely, D., Gneezy, U., Loewenstein, G. and Mazar, N. (2009). Large Stakes and Big Mistakes. *Review of Economic Studies*, [online] 76(2), pp.451-469. Available at: https://rady.ucsd.edu/faculty/directory/gneezy/pub/docs/large-stakes.pdf [Accessed 4 Jun. 2019].

Practical steps to overcome the effects of pressure on performance (Step 18).

Arsal, G., Eccles, D. and Ericsson, K. (2016). Cognitive mediation of putting: Use of a think-aloud measure and implications for studies of golf-putting in the laboratory. *Psychology of Sport and Exercise*, 27, pp.18-27.

The word "saccade" for eye movements apparently coined by French ophthalmologist Émile Javal (Step 20).

Javal, É. (1878). *"Essai sur la physiologie de la lecture"*. [online] Pure.mpg.de. Available in French at: https://pure.mpg.de/rest/items/item_2350899/compon ent/file_2350898/content [Accessed 4 Jun. 2019].

Significantly more students get answers right when key words in a question are emphasised with bold typeface (Step 20).

Sweiry, E., Crisp, V., Ahmed, A. and Pollitt, A. (2002). Tales of the expected: The influence of students' expectations on exam validity. In: *Annual Conference of the British Educational Research Association*. [online] University of Cambridge Local Examinations Syndicate. Available at: http://www.leeds.ac.uk/educol/documents/00002543.h tm [Accessed 4 Jun. 2019].

Spreading activation theory of memory (Step 25).

Collins, A. and Loftus, E. (1975). A spreading-activation theory of semantic processing. *Psychological Review*, 82(6), pp.407-428.

Evidence for the benefits of guessing in negatively-marked multiple choice papers (Step 26).

Hammond, E., McIndoe, A., Sansome, A. and Spargo, P. (1998). Multiple-choice examinations: adopting an evidence-based approach to exam technique. *Anaesthesia*, [online] 53(11), pp.1105-1108. Available at: https://onlinelibrary.wiley.com/doi/full/10.1046/j.1365-2044.1998.00583.x [Accessed 4 Jun. 2019].

Suggested reading

The following books have provided inspiration or information for Outsmart Your Exams.

Beilock, S. (2011). *Choke*. New York: Atria Books.

Cottrell, S. (2012) *Exam skills handbook - achieving peak performance*. London: Palgrave Macmillan.

Duckworth, A. (2018). *Grit*. New York: Scribner Book Company.

Dweck, C. (2017). *Mindset*. London: Robinson.

Hunt-Davis, B. and Beveridge, H. (2011). *Will it make the boat go faster?* Leicester: Troubador.

Gawande, A. (2009). *The Checklist Manifesto*. New York: Metropolitan Books.

Salles, D. (2017). *The Mr Salles guide to 100% in AQA English language GCSE*. Woodbridge: John Catt Educational Ltd.

Sutherland, S. (2013). Irrationality. London: Pinter & Martin Ltd.

Walker, M. (2018). *Why we sleep*. New York: Scribner Book Company.

These final books are recommended not so much because of what they have to say about exam technique, but because they are among my favourite books for learning how to improve your study and revision skills, helping ensure that by the time exam day rolls round, you are as well-prepared as you possibly can be. You can find all of these recommendations and more at examstudyexpert.com/bookshelf.

Brown, P., McDaniel, M. and Roediger, H. (2014). *Make It Stick*. Cambridge: Harvard University Press.

Clear, J. (2018). *Atomic Habits*. London: Random House Business Books.

Ericsson, A. (2017). *Peak*. New York: Vintage.

Oakley, B. (2014). *A Mind for Numbers*. New York: Tarcher.

Newport, C. (2005). *How to Win at College*. New York: Broadway Books.

Newport, C. (2016). *Deep Work: Rules for Focused Success in a Distracted World*. London: Piatkus.

Weinstein, Y., Sumeracki, M. and Caviglioli, O. (2018). *Understanding How We Learn*. Abingdon: Routledge.

ACKNOWLEDGEMENTS

I'd been gathering exam tips, and writing them down for over 10 years before I took the plunge and drew them together into this book.

In those years, I reckon I've spent around 300 hours sat in an exam room, and the majority of my pre-adult life preparing for the next round of exams, first at school, then at uni. Suffice it to say, exams were a big part of my life!

Finally producing this book has been quite a milestone for me, for which I owe a great debt of thanks to many people.

I'd like to thank my wife and best friend, Diana, for always being there for me, for listening to my endless ideas about this project, and for editing the original draft of this manuscript in record time.

I'd like to thank my parents, for their encouragement, wisdom and support – and for going to the ends of the earth to help me get through my exams when I was young. I couldn't have done any of this without you. Thanks too to my brother, Henry – always ready to bring me back to earth, and always a true friend.

I owe a debt to the people who inspired me to exam success: Richard Berengarten, Margaret Stanley, Peter Roberts, Dave Thompson, Dave Merrick, Gordon Prescott, Anne Stanyon, Jonathan Morris, John Bell and so many besides. My gratitude too to the lecturers at Cambridge's Experimental Psychology Department who kindled my passion for how the brain works: Brian Little, Lisa Saksida, Tim Bussey, Greg Davis, Mike Aitken, Jon Simons.

Thank you to the people I could look to for counsel and inspiration over the years: Margaret Stanley, Paul Bryan, Diana Bushby, Emily Taylor, Aron Schleider, Alex Vinall, Joachim Cassel, Freddie Tapner, Davina Barron, Adam Wood, James Slimings, Nick Gebbett, Aled Walker, Jeremy Hamilton, Nick Wheeler-Robinson, Christopher Woods.

And to my old exam-season friends and allies in and around the Plumb Auditorium at Christ's College: Matt Tsim, Laura Wharton, Amy Puttick, Nathan Gower, Rob King, Johnny Basset, Alex Lit, Ruth Dewhurst, Maeve O'Dwyer, Christabel Rose, Holly East, Will Critchlow, Vicky Pinion, Sabrina Bezza, Rob Stiff, William Wallis, Tom Gilliver, Megan Riddington, Amy Paterson, Alex Greaves, George Wild, Richard Mifsud. I didn't always believe it at the time, but it turns out, you were right all along: there were no limits.

Printed in Great Britain
by Amazon

39410494R00096